"*America is always at its best when it hears from its young and helps make their dreams come true. 'Freedom's Answer' is the message of America's newest dreamers. It will move you - and the country.*"
President Gerald R. Ford

"*This is a remarkable story written by a group of high school students who decided in the wake of 9/11 to confront, and try to change, the cynicism that has grown up around American politics. And, they have come up with a bold plan to do it.*"
Bob Schieffer,
CBS News Chief Washington Correspondent

"*Often, in the most difficult periods in our history, it is the nation's youth who have inspired America to live up to its ideals. Freedom's Answer deserves great credit for doing so today - young Americans serving America well, reminding all our people of the profound and very practical importance of the right to vote as the path to the kind of nation we want to be in the years ahead.*"
Senator Edward M. Kennedy

"*If these young patriots are successful, we will all enjoy a brighter future. They're America at its very best. Join them! Help them! They're making history!*"
Mary Matalin
Former Senior Advisor to Vice President Cheney

"*Freedom's Answer is an inspiring story about how a group of students most too young to vote... strengthened our democracy in the midst of perilous times.*"
Governor Christine Todd Whitman

"*Freedom's Answer gives young people an excellent way of contributing to American democracy.*"
President Jimmy Carter

Freedom's Answer

*When the Twin Towers fell,
the next generation rose!*

By the September 11 Generation

Little Moose Press
269 South Beverly Blvd., #1065
Beverly Hills, CA 90212
Phone: 310-278-6237 Fax: 310-278-6238
Toll Free: 866-234-0626
Email: info@littlemoosepress.com
www.littlemoosepress.com

First edition
Printed in the United States of America
ISBN 0-9720227-7-5
Library of Congress Control Number: 2003111725
Publisher's Cataloging-In-Publication available upon request.

TO AMERICA'S
NEWEST DREAMERS

The Next Great Generation?

Freedom's Answer is the story of what teens from across the country accomplished though they were too young to vote and had none of the money that funds the rest of politics. This book chronicles how students of all nationalities, religions and political persuasions breathed life into a vision, made it real, and now it calls readers to action, asking them to expand the dream.

The September 11 Generation has something that most recent generations do not. We have vivid, living pictures of the magnificence of the human spirit manifested in the acts of heroism in the "Second Moment" of September 11th, the acts of brotherhood and unity that could be the defining moment of our generation and our country.

These were not manufactured dramas, they were spontaneous real life occurrences captured on videotape, aired and burned into our psyches. Strangers comforted distraught souls hoping against hope for word of relatives believed to have been in the Twin Towers, firemen traveled cross country at their own expense to lend a hand, executives with grimy suits and loosened ties carried coffee cups to rescue workers amidst the rubble night after night.

This is not airy idealism, it is the solid stuff of reality; it is America at its best. It is the reality of compassion and cooperation that we will create.

Engagement is the lifeblood of a democratic political system. Disengagement from it is the reality of recent generations. Re-engagement is the message and method of Freedom's Answer. It is more than a story; it is a roadmap to gaining empowerment in our system, and therefore in our country, our world, and our future.

This book is about what answer freedom (and a million high schools students who revere it) provided in the election of 2002 to the terrorism of 2001. Millions more will write the next chapter of Freedom's Answer in 2004 - and re-write how our democracy works. <u>That is our American Dream.</u>

About the Authors

The book before you belongs to our generation. No adult conceived it, outlined it, organized it, or wrote it. It is the product of kids who begged each other not to forget what happened when they dared to dream. The authors are guys and girls - black and white - northern and southern - urban and rural - seniors and sophomores - liberals and conservatives - hawks and doves - young and younger still.

Zach Clayton of Broughton High School in Raleigh, North Carolina and Puneet Gambhir of Thomas Jefferson High School in Alexandria, Virginia steered the conception and development of Freedom's Answer. With the help of Washington's Dane Anderson, New York's Lindsay Ullman, South Dakota's Victoria Zoellner, and Maryland's Bernard Holloway, the team of six spent five months co-authoring the book via telephone, email, and two face-to-face visits. Through seven hundred interviews and thousands of pages of transcribed notes, the students captured the stories of nearly two thousand young Americans.

Contents

Foreword

U.S. Supreme Court Justice Louis Brandeis once said, "The only title in our democracy superior to that of President is the title of citizen."

At the Department of Education, we take that as a serious challenge every day. One of the primary roles of America's public education system is to prepare young people not only with the skills and knowledge to pursue their own American dream, but also with a firm understanding of their duties and responsibilities as citizens to each other and to our country.

The strength of a nation begins in the classroom, with students learning about the ideals of freedom upon which our great nation was built, love of country, and the selfless sacrifice of those who have answered the call to defend it. By their own admission, it took the tragic events of September 11th to catch the attention of many in the generation of the young people who wrote this book and make them realize their own civic responsibility. But once they saw what they could do to make a difference, they became engaged and they learned important lessons in the process.

They learned that there is no limit to what you can do if you set high goals and then work hard to achieve them. And they learned how Americans - no matter how young or old - can be a powerful force for change if they band together in common purpose for a common good.

Young people are often told that they are our future, and that is true. But they are also our here and now.

The story of the September 11 Generation is an inspirational call to arms for other young people to stand up and be counted as present and engaged and focused on the future, starting with the here and now.

Rod Paige
U.S. Secretary of Education

After the Shock

Your third period gym class in Florida stopped exercising. The school library closed in Illinois. You jumped out of bed in California because you heard your mom screaming.

Shrieks pierced the still of morning Pentagon routines and the bustling streets of New York halted as people clung to each other, faces aghast, watching concrete collapse and inverted steel beams tumble.

A thick plume of black smoke marred the pastel blues of the picturesque Pennsylvania sky. Quaint barns and crumbling farm fences quickly lost their innocence as serenity slipped from the crisp September morning, stolen by terror. The idyllic Somerset County scene, which could have been a Norman Rockwell painting at 9:00, was cruelly transformed into a twisted action film by 10:00.

But the cameramen weren't from Warner Brothers and the backdrop wasn't a Studio Six set. CNN and ABC taped New York and DC; the actors were real and we were terrified viewer-participants, desperately dialing family cell phones while watching smoke probe into every crevice of vacuous New York City space. Disgust, contempt, disbelief, amazement roiled the nation. You winced while watching some collegiate brunette uncontrollably sob in the streets of DC, you trembled when you heard rumors that planes were heading for the White House, you were empty when you watched rescue workers unload body bags by the dozen in front of the Towers.

We don't have to describe the numbing pain of watching New York City and our nation's capital burn. You were there, beside us, connected with open eyes and tender hearts as we crowded in clusters around TVs, watching a shocked Jennings and Brokaw fumble for words which would adequately express the emotion we all felt, but couldn't convey.

The country changed, the world changed, and we witnessed it live on TV. New York, our jeweled capital of commerce, was engulfed in flames and the Pentagon, that revered and impenetrable icon of American military supremacy, seemed oddly vulnerable. The country bled together, cried together, watched bodies fall from the sky together. The thing about 9-11 was that it was happening to us. It was happening to you, to me, and we weren't quite sure what was happening next. It was live, riveting, and we couldn't escape it. Nobody could look at the pictures and not feel hollow.

The pain was unsettling, it made our bodies ache and our hearts crumble. We were confused, caught in an inexorable flow of mixed emotions. You wanted to be alone and you craved to be with those you loved, you were proud and mortified, but most of all you were scared. Loss and pain emanated from distant stares, and we endured this silent gut-wrenching insecurity as we clung to each other. Our foundation had been rocked, everything we trusted and believed was tossed out the window… it was the plague, it was a holocaust, it was the worst within human nature.

The Second Moment of 9-11

So what happened in the immediate aftermath of the terror was all the more startling, because after witnessing the depths of hatred, after feeling physically sick from the devastation, we saw acts of extraordinary love. Valiant firemen forged up 80 flights of stairs while everyone else hurried down. Medics sprinted to Ground Zero aiding the injured thousands. Cops stood beneath shaking buildings, warning away passersby. And it wasn't just their heroism, their selflessness, it was the love the city had for them and for their sacrifice and for those they never knew who jumped to their death or who had been crushed to death simply for being there. The city came together. A city that rarely came together for anybody or anything came together.

Marketing executives left their jobs to volunteer, attorneys came ready to mop floors and serve food, people lined up around the block to give blood. Our President flanked the flag atop a scarred fire truck in the midst of still smoldering rubble while dogs and their handlers probed on for survivors. Charitable contributions poured in, we clogged the streets with candles, we said prayers in a thousand tongues. And the attack filled with hatred produced a response brimming with love as we treated victims and embraced our heroes.

If New Yorkers could rise above pettiness and act out of love, so could a nation. We were inspired because after witnessing the worst of humankind, we saw its best. The rescuers didn't rush into crumbling buildings seeking a bigger bonus or better ratings or 15 minutes of fame. They did it because they could, because they were compelled to. They did it because it is what free people do when they suddenly realize that their freedom is going. They unite to save it. Again and again, they went back into hell seeking to save the lives and dignity of those whose freedom had been taken, risking and sometimes giving it all.

September twelfth, we were uplifted by flags on mailboxes, windows painted with red, white, and blue, and car headlights turned on, an act of national solidarity and remembrance. Superficial differences became trivial, because for an instant, we were too dumbfounded to worry about race, class or gender. We paused for a collective moment, talking to everyone, watching the news side-by-side, ignoring even our own carefully crafted high school cliques. Neighbors congregated in circles clutching candles, churches held special services, the camaraderie was overwhelming. Those who never cried, mourned; those who never gave, acted.

This counter-attack of compassion was the second moment of 9-11, a shining one. From the ruins and ashes of fallen buildings arose the September 11 Generation. We, that fiery group of web-based teens born in the last two decades, were transformed from the overlooked younger siblings of Gen X into those connected by the second moment of 9-11. Those who came before us watched Kennedy assassinated, the Challenger explode, and the Gulf War in the living room.

Untempered by such previous calamity, we are defined by a different episode, one that will forever remain trapped in our minds. It's more personal than the radio's crackling which bore news of a bombing in Pearl Harbor, more believable than watching a fuzzy black and white tape of a President being shot, and certainly more concentrated than any of our post-WWII military conflicts. Even Vietnam was *there*; this was *here*.

The September 11 Generation is a title that doesn't represent the attack, but rather the heroic response. We came of age when we saw neighbors invite displaced residents into their homes - and volunteers fly in from around the country - and the bravery and selflessness of the firemen. We all wanted to be them. We all wished we had their courage, their selflessness, their instinctive love of their fellowman that caused them to do the unthinkable - to risk, often to give, everything they had. That is what pulled the nation together, a monumental willingness to sacrifice for others, a passion we all felt and somehow wished that we could match - and still do.

We're the new kids on the block, the ones who have grown up with computers in the classroom but teachers who don't know how to use them. And the experts estimate we have over 100 million members. They say that we're better taken care of, we're more ambitious, and we're less likely to use drugs than our parents. Our grandparents wore cardboard in their shoes during the Great Depression, our dads duked it out in the heat of Vietnamese jungles - and most of us struggle merely with questions like "Will I get accepted to my dream school?" Life is good, or at least pretty good, because we're exhausted from soccer practice and piano lessons instead of child labor. We commit fewer crimes than Gen X did; we have fewer after-school jobs but less free time; and generational historians Neil Howe and Bill Strauss say, we're "…perhaps destined to dominate the twenty-first century like today's fading and ennobled G.I. Generation dominated the twentieth." We could become the next great generation.

Yet there is a problem: we are jaded when it comes to politics. We're willing to serve soup at the soup kitchen, but we are not quite ready to serve on the board of directors. We read about the Constitution, the Bill of Rights, and voting, but there is some gross disconnect between the honor of our founders and the present system of politics. Community service? Fine, hey - it's even a requirement at some schools, but mock elections, government, patriotism - why bother, "it's not for me." Or at least that used to be the attitude. Now, our classroom discussions of current events seem to have taken on new urgency. We even find ourselves glancing over the headlines before we hit the sports page and "citizenship" means just a little bit more. James Madison once called our union "the hope of liberty throughout the world," and in the aftermath of 9-11 we found ourselves nodding along with him.

Sure, we're pessimistic - TV tells us to be, our parents tell us to be, even our textbooks tell us to be. Yet, isn't there some promise in the rebirth, in the unity, that we witnessed the morning of September 12?

The tragedy made clear how much our country depends on the active spirit of citizenship and community - how much we suffer if we don't have it, how many problems we can solve if we exercise it, how vulnerable we are if we don't express it, and how dangerous it is if outsiders perceive that we lack it. When we don't use this spirit, it atrophies. To keep alive this spirit, what was a better idea than America's youngest reminding the country to vote?

So we latched onto a proposal that Doug Bailey, a former Republican political strategist, and Mike McCurry, President Clinton's past press secretary, presented to students around the nation. The two men - both extraordinarily innovative political thinkers - found themselves asking the same question many Americans were: "How could we summon post 9-11 desire to do something for the common good into an idea that would make our democracy better?" Answering the call was a group of a dozen students who united to lead a movement called Freedom's Answer. We were idealistic, brimming with optimism - ready to tackle the apathy that infested our own schools and communities even as the political leaders at home and in Washington remained terminally unconvinced that a kid could make a difference. Our objective was to revamp the way students felt about government and to raise turnout in the 2002 election to new levels - record levels.

We would flood our neighbors and relatives with requests to vote, prompting them to make it to the polls, never once saying "Register Democrat" or "Vote Republican." Our announced goal: to break the national voting record in a non-presidential election year. It would be the first national effort to encourage students under eighteen to actually participate in the real election process, and if we did it right, we would create the largest non-partisan voter turnout effort ever. Imagine that! Students too young to vote trying to break a voter turnout record.

When the cynics found out it was us, students, who wanted to do the work, some laughed, some didn't even care enough to do that. After all, the goal was huge and the McCurry-Bailey team had tried to get in high schools before, with an online project called Youth-e-Vote. The mock election concept hadn't taken - most principals had shirked at the idea of a school-wide internet endeavor, and the effort was adult-run, adult-led. This time McCurry-Bailey figured, they'd count on us - the high school students - to make it work.

Tragedy made us pay attention and when we looked around we saw sacrifices by Washington, Jefferson, Lincoln, Roosevelt, and King which established an inheritance of freedom, a birthright that both soldiers and firemen have died to defend, and a legacy we were obligated to protect. 9-11 could be more than defining, it could be a transforming moment in our history, one that could propel our generation to action. So we joined together hoping to change America, not old enough to vote, not sure where we'd go to college, but committed to rallying the generation to new greatness. We'd fight for freedom the only way we could, by asking America to exercise its most basic right - by asking America to vote.

Why Some Said "Impossible"

In 1960, 68.8 million adults voted and 40.8 million didn't; in 1996, 96.3 million adults voted and 100.2 million didn't. Imagine that: less than half of eligible voters elected our President.

Unfortunately, people who don't vote are not as deeply invested in our system of democracy. Americans are half as likely to attend a campaign rally, work for a party or contribute to a candidate as they were 30 years ago. Politicians are getting larger checks from a smaller group, votes from fewer people, and when they do go out to campaign, they're seeing more of the same faces. Normal folks are just giving up on the entire system altogether. And most of those giving up are the members of Generation X. In fact, a recent study by Harvard University, the Washington Post, and the Henry J. Kaiser Family Foundation predicted that by 2022 the number of adults over 65 who vote will exceed young adults by 4 to 1. In 2000, 68% of those over 65 voted and 68% of those between 18 and 25 didn't.

On the whole, Americans seem to be taking the blessings of liberty more seriously than the responsibilities. The average amount of time spent watching the two national political conventions has dropped from twenty-five hours to three over the past half-century. Debate watching has plummeted as well; Thomas Patterson, author of <u>Vanishing Voter</u>, noted that WWF's *SmackDown* had 4 times as many viewers as the first Democratic debate in 2000. The Rock smashing chairs on people's heads beats picking the leader of the free world?

The civic-minded generation raised during the Depression and the Second World War has been gradually replaced by the more private-minded Boomer and X generations that lived through childhood and adolescence without having experienced a great single national crisis. As a result, today's young adults are less politically interested and informed than any cohort of new voters on record. In 2000 alone, there were 30 million missing voters under 30.

Why? The quality of campaigns doesn't help turnout. Consultants think it's more cost effective to persuade voters to dislike a candidate than to like him and target certain groups with negative ads to "deep-freeze" their turnout. Less civics is taught in schools and the end of the draft has decreased civic duty. To our grandparents, the draft was a legal obligation that every family and every young man had to recognize. Today's all-volunteer army removes the likelihood of mandatory military service for our generation, but it also means we have never had to think deeply about what sacrifice means.

The biggest problem may be cynicism among educators and the media. Introductory government classes in college and high school are taught with uninspiring books, like Thomas Dye's <u>Politics in America</u>, which calls personal ambition the driving force in politics: "Politics attracts people for whom power and celebrity mean recognition, which is more rewarding than money, leisure, or privacy." In short, we are taught that many politicians are self-serving liars constantly striving to downplay their ambition.

So we'll enter college having taken fewer civics classes than any modern generation on record, then read in our first class on government that soft money and hard money are the only realities, and that our vote won't really matter.

No wonder most voters say they hate campaigns. As Washington journalist David Broder remarks, "Cynicism is epidemic right now. It saps people's confidence in politics and public officials, and it erodes both the standing and standards of journalism. If the assumption is that nothing is on the level, nothing is what it seems, then citizenship becomes a game for fools, and there is no point in trying to stay informed."

The media doesn't help. Curtis Gans, Director of the Center for Voting and Democracy, calls "television, cable, satellite and the Internet" a "profound" reason why we don't vote. Whether you are watching The Late Show or The Simpsons - politicians are invariably subjected to ridicule. The ratings game rule dictates bad news over good, prompting commentator Michael Robinson to say, "If you don't have anything bad to say about someone, don't say anything at all."

So we tune out. We volunteer at food banks and homeless shelters, but we don't participate politically.

But unfortunately, when people ignore politicians - politicians ignore them. The 18-25 age group has the lowest rate of participation of any group in the country, so politicians don't have to count on our support to be elected. The young don't vote, so the politicians don't listen, so the young don't vote, so the politicians don't listen... It's a self-defeating cycle - for freedom and for us. It's time to break it.

The Dry Wood

We could accept the status quo, we could watch from the sidelines, griping along with the chorus of the apathetic and cynical. But are we really doing ourselves, our community, or America much good by hanging around complaining? For years, ordinary teens around the country have been quietly waiting for some galvanizing movement to ignite action. Some are student body presidents, some uninvolved freshman. Most, like Sky DeBeover of North Carolina, ask hard questions. "In student council, we always talk about how to build a better prom. Why don't we ask, 'how can we build a better America'?"

Other student leaders like Connecticut's Ben Erwin weigh in. "Every school has talented leaders. Every community has kids who have the ability to make a change. But do they go out and do it?" The answer shows whether or not your club, your team, or your school is fulfilling its potential. A.J. Singletary, from Arkansas, knows well the difficulties of motivating students in his rural high school. The primary dilemma he sees is energizing capable but unmotivated kids. "You just have to convince them to start." The problem is arousing the potential initiators scattered around the country, compelling them to begin and continue.

There has never been a shortage of teens in our generation willing to "make a difference." Super-kids like Canada's Craig Keilburger, who started an international child labor protest before his fourteenth birthday, are offered as certifiable proof of our generation's commitment to community service. After all, recent studies released by the Pew Charitable Trusts indicate that our generation is more altruistic than either Gen X or the Boomers.

Tim Lehan, a senior at Raleigh's Broughton High School, personifies that change. He's angry "National Honor Society allows students to pay $10 to buy a book instead of actually asking them to read it to a child." That was okay for Gen X, he says, "…but I think we want more. We want to give back and feel the difference." It's a matter of approach. "I want hands-on projects, stuff that you can't buy. Asking dad for ten bucks just to meet some club requirement cheapens the value of service."

Tim isn't voicing an unusual sentiment. His class-mate, freshman Sandy Roberts, sees eye-to-eye, "Nobody thinks big; no one quotes Churchill anymore. I want our generation to persuade America to think in terms of an idea or cause that is bigger than its own agenda." This chiseled cross-country runner isn't foolish enough to dismiss some individuals' apathy, but he's not pessimistic enough to think their lethargy can't be overcome. "I'm tired of being called Gen X; we're not Gen X. We have our own weaknesses and strengths...but we are children and young adults of a new era." He's right and that means a dazzling array of possibilities exists.

Stress, lack of time, and other normal adolescent struggles make it hard for us to believe we can change the world. But we don't have to do it all after school. We do it piece-by-piece, linked with the rest of our school, state, and nation. Making small inroads, we convince others that we care about the community and that they should also. Gradually attitudes transform. After all, history is nothing but the process of changing ideas and faces.

Laura Gingrich, a bite-sized farm girl from Iowa with long blonde hair and a 24-7 smile, wasn't so sure initial-ly, "I was uncertain how much power I could have. Government seems so distant sometimes." And she is right. Because most of us have never fully exercised our power to shape community affairs, we don't know where the real boundaries lie. Continuing, she says:

> The easiest part though, is believing your efforts are worthwhile once you've begun. Because you make a difference once, you make a difference

twice, you do it again and people's heads pop out
and they start to ask what is happening. Young
people (even too young to vote) can have an
impact on our political process. Eventually even
the politicians catch on and maybe, just maybe,
they should start listening to us.

Our high schools have been evolving over the past
years as the generation shift has occurred, and every project, each attempt at stirring our communities, has added a
splash of lighter fluid to a growing stack of fuel. Henry
Foust, a longtime student council advisor from a rural
senior high, describes the metamorphosis. "All of a sudden, you have kids here who are saying 'let's stop playing
at leadership - let's do something that will change lives
and communities.'" Then it just becomes a matter of
rousing support behind them, because we're squandering
our potential if we aren't leading, if we aren't pushing forward. Sky DeBeover jumps back in, "The dances and
pep-rallies are fun, but at the end of the day what impact
do they leave?" That is the line in the sand separating
Gen X and the September 11 Generation - the complacent
replaced by the dreamers. We, the visionaries, were dry
wood, waiting for a spark.

The Spark

Before September 11, students were already jump-
starting local efforts in communities - pioneering
attempts to elect a student to the school board, build a
park across the street, and lobby legislators for a school
bond. But it wasn't widespread. You heard a story here,
saw a news piece there, all begging the question: What
would it take to ignite such potential nationwide? We

were holding our breath, ready but not sure where the next step would take us. Then terror struck. Towers down, planes crashing, army activated, war coming... the country was changing. We were too. Anna Freidinger, a blue-eyed senior from Illinois, recalled her own reaction to the attacks:

> One girl's mom was going to DC that morning and our whole class was trying to comfort her because she was so worried. It shocked me, bringing me out of the mindset that when we're in America we're safe. At marching band practice the next day we were practicing the Star Spangled Banner for the football game and there was a student who drove across the nearby street with a flag waving out the back of the truck and there was just some kind of understanding. Communities came together. We had a town prayer so that everyone could have a shoulder to lean on.

Due east in New Hampshire, John Ouellette was sitting in his Spanish II class when a fellow classmate came running into the room gasping that the World Trade Centers and the Pentagon had been attacked. "All of us ran to the student to find out as much information from him as possible," he said. A somber, shocked mood settled upon the school as he stumbled to his third block class, American Studies. "All of the students were talking about what they had heard and exchanging information with one another, trying to understand what had happened to our nation. Right in front of me on TV, two airplanes hit the World Trade Centers. Another hit the Pentagon. Tears flowed from my eyes as more questions burst into my head."

Tears flowed into many of our eyes, even streaming

down the made-up cheeks of the guys on TV. Jon Stewart, The Daily Show's irreverent news-anchor, bit his lip as he sniffled through an eloquent memoriam. "Any fool can blow something up. Any fool can destroy. But to see these guys, these firefighters, these policemen and people from all over the country, literally, with buckets rebuilding. That's extraordinary. That's why we've already won. It's light. It's democracy. They can't shut that down." Stewart, usually known for his "back-of-the-class" antics at press conferences and for pestering politicians with biting sarcasm continued:

> The view from my apartment was the World Trade Center and now it's gone. They attacked it. This symbol of American ingenuity and strength and labor and imagination and commerce and it is gone. But you know what the view is now? The Statue of Liberty. The view from the south of Manhattan is now the Statue of Liberty. You can't beat that.

It was that indefatigable optimism that captured our spirits, that permeated our hearts. We couldn't avoid the aftermath of 9-11, we couldn't escape the beauty of human nature's triumph. Camaraderie and benevolence got the last word in and America loved every minute of it.

Soham Dave of Maryland concurred. He said that September 11 forged a common character, enriching our innate desire to give back in a real way. "We didn't want to play a 'mock election' game; we wanted something serious to improve the country. There haven't been many things worth struggling for which our generation has had an opportunity to fight."

André Jennings, a Maryland senior, said the attacks

instilled in him a new attitude, *carpe diem*. "Before 9-11, I thought service was important," he told us, "but I didn't really do anything. Afterwards, I realized I didn't have the luxury of waiting." André's father, who works in the Pentagon, survived - but a lot of his friends did not. The lesson gleaned from such close proximity to the devastation? "It makes me take life more seriously. Don't wait to do something, just act when you feel the inspiration."

Across the country students opened up, speaking to us hesitantly at conferences or on the phone, pausing awkwardly as they stammered out their feelings. The emotions were real, and they wanted to respond, to improve the country they no longer could take for granted. Lawrence Green of Charleston, South Carolina, an all-star athlete in three sports, was overwhelmed with the outpouring of patriotism. "September 11 brought us out of our bubble. And when we finally looked around we saw that the world of adults was not infallible. They weren't doing fine without us; they never even stopped to consider that maybe we were saying something worth listening to."

Before 9-11, the question was "what can we do?" The answers were evasive: "I have to have permission to stay out past 11:30... Me?? I'm 16; I'm not powerful... I don't have secretaries and expense accounts, video conferencing, and 37th floor meetings... I HAVE TO GET A PASS TO GO TO THE BATHROOM!!" But the firefighters didn't make excuses, the President didn't accept justifications, and the country certainly didn't need either. Could we rise to a heightened challenge? Could we convert our longstanding desire to act into national progress?

The Fire

Teens around the country woke up, threw on the Clearasil, and evaluated themselves and their communities. Some of it was a growing maturity... we were finally in high school, becoming independent, capable of fighting for our convictions, but much of it was prompted by our coming of age experience, 9-11. Calamity wasn't new; we had witnessed Columbine, even Oklahoma City. Yet, then we didn't feel like the events were happening to us. We were far younger anyhow and while tragic, the events didn't saturate the national consciousness; they weren't an assault against the nation. 9-11 was that assault, an awful, contemptible crime against New York, Pennsylvania, Washington, and America. A week later we hadn't returned to normalcy: airports were different, people were stirred, and nationalism was ubiquitous.

We looked in the mirror and were forced to choose between action and inaction. So we sent our dollar to the Afghani Children's Foundation like the President asked and did a coin drive for the September 11 Fund. Maybe we made cards for a high school nearby one of the crash sites, or dropped bottled water off at the local Salvation Army. Whatever it was, it was sincerely offered, but not completely fulfilling... in fact - far from fulfilling. The urgency, the proximity, the reality of watching the buildings fall in front of our eyes bred an intimacy which meant sending someone a postcard would never suffice.

A gaping canyon spanned the distance between the emotional impact of the attacks and our actual efforts to assist in the recovery. In the midst of a fierce rescue effort we were supposed to meagerly offer only a buck to Afghani children whose lives would be destroyed by war? Wait. Pause. Maybe there was more. In fact, certainly there was more. Hadn't Bush called the attack on freedom "an attack on the ideals that make us a nation?"

Then it hit us. The President didn't ask Adult America for donations to aid Afghanistan; he specifically asked the children to help. He gave us a role, saying there are other ways to fight terror than to be in the Army; he asked us to show the "goodness of America" through fighting evil with "kindness and love and compassion." We were called to a mission, told that we could achieve something on our own. Giving a buck was no big deal, but in the aftermath of the attacks we heard our names being called, summoned to a larger national task. The spark was being nurtured. Couldn't we do more, couldn't we go a step further… push the limit? Our first stab at an answer wasn't monumental or even inspiring and we knew it. The right response to counter that harrowing catastrophe had to capture the imagination, push into an unexplored avenue, negate the attacker's cowardice with our boldness. We would build a new monument. A tower so tall it would captivate the nation like two towers had once done to the steadily ambitious Manhattan skyline. We would break the national voter turnout record.

Historians would inevitably write that the Twin Towers of New York fell on 9-11. But would they also write that the Twin Towers of America, freedom and the right to vote, would never fall? Could we author that chapter, alter the course of democracy? What the hell, we had nothing to lose.

Ambitious? Quite. Impractical? Perhaps. But possible? The world may not have thought so, but we knew better. Through some combination of generational readiness and post-9-11 introspection, we became determined to impact the process by which we elect our leaders.

A million reasons motivated students to activism, to participate in Freedom's Answer - but the kids basically boiled down to two categories. Scott Clayton was one, someone wanting to act, but not sure where to start. "When I was in the 5th grade, our youth minister died of AIDS," he began. "Why didn't the church youth, who loved this man, who cared for this man, who literally day-by-day watched him die, do something? They appreciated him, but they never connected the dots to remember him with more than words and tears. Did I volunteer, help with the AIDS Walk, something... anything?" he wistfully asks. "No. So to see kids my age leading by example, pushing to do what they think is right, hit a nerve. And I didn't want to miss another opportunity."

Meredith Smith from South Carolina was another, pushed into action by the attacks. Her take: "When America was violated on her own soil, the people of America reacted with patriotism and determination. Freedom's Answer captured that emotion."

Sure, some kids were always going to be interested in this stuff, but Scott and Meredith were two key constituencies we had to engage to spread the project beyond the ordinary suspects - Teenage Democrat and Young Conservative Clubs. They were the middle ground - the 80% who vacillate between dual extremes of activism and apathy. Convincing them was the only way we would have the numbers to succeed.

It seemed the generation was standing by, waiting to give back to their communities. But the one common denominator every kid brought to the table? A healthy respect for the student ownership. Dane Anderson, an articulate west-coaster, called student ownership "the first and most important principle of the project." Freedom's Answer would fly or fail based on our willingness to pour our hearts and souls into it.

That student-ownership inspired Darla Phillips. She was impressed to see kids rallying together for anything. "The sad part about 9-11 is that it took a tragedy for America to respect and be thankful for our country."

Moving Forward

Thousands of voices chimed in, each ready to make his or her own contribution. The result: a beautiful patch-work of perspective that, when woven together, changed American voter turnout in 2002. Infinitesimal threads entwined scattered geography, ethnicity, and politics into an astonishing tapestry.

Clubs, sports, grades… at times we've all felt like we were living our lives for other people. But Freedom's Answer wasn't designed for a resume, it was our chance to cultivate our own piece of democracy. No "B+" for college, no goal for the soccer coach, or room cleaned for your mom, just the fulfillment of crafting your own square and connecting it to the others. Right now, we're laden with college applications, endless English papers, and the list goes on. But after that, those worries become graduate school or meeting deadlines for your first full-time job or taking care of the kids and pretty soon life passes by in a blurry cycle. The question became inevitable: at the end of the year didn't we want to leave the world with something more than a busy schedule?

In our hearts we believed in something larger than any one of us, greater than any party or person - we believed in America as she can be, as she should be. We aspired to write a new page of history, heralding an exultant effort which reinvigorated the country. For too long our generation has lacked real vision, missed true leadership, has been blind to the possibility that our power can make a difference. The cynics indeed scoffed, as they always do, but they once laughed at Bill Gates for dropping out of college and scowled at Jefferson when he talked about "all men are created equal." You arrive at greatness by refusing to accept the status quo, by damning the critics and plowing onward, by gazing at the horizon and chasing the setting sun.

Ordinary people can make extraordinary things happen. We found that out, even before our senior prom. This book is a testament to that, and a witness to the power of an idea. It's a book we had to write - because everyone who has ever longed to generate change needs to know that there are no limits. Because everyone who feels sympathy towards action but doesn't take the next step looks back at some point and regrets it.

The Kids Came Out

Chapter 2

Thunder erupted from the downcast sky, electricity pulsating through the blood of the dreamers. Rain, blasting the cement sidewalks, ushered the special guests into the sanctuary of 529 14th Street NW, Washington D.C, thirteenth floor - The National Press Club. These elite of the non-profit world brushed the beads of water off their Gucci coats and marched through the elevator doors. They had come to meet us: five high school students, prepared to deliver.

We arrived that morning. Our generation arrived. For years, the crushing weight of apathy, cynicism and disbelief oppressed the energy of our dormant generation. But an alarm had blared and we arose. With a newfound sense of place, we were spewing ideas, searching for ownership, and passionately wanting a vision. We were searching for our complement, a cause worthy of our idealism.

The non-profit political rajas, who had ventured through the soggy mess, listened to the dream being unfurled before them. High school students. High school students triggering a record voter turnout in an off-year election, to prove that American democracy had not retreated to the nursing home. Freedom's Answer was alive and primed to hit the streets. Doug Bailey, his long white hair combed back, and a flushed

Mike McCurry revealed their brainchild. They came ready to spark an idea, to begin a new page of history, but they also came ready to let go... ready to watch us take over.

Grey-Haired "Allies"

The spectators sitting with us at our first press conference were nice enough. We were all tickled to see them show up that morning and beamed as they wished us the best of luck, gave us the names of their secretaries, and left. But progressively we discerned a sharp split in the quality of adult: they were either one of the few visionaries - standing in formation with Bailey and McCurry - or in the crowd of the cynics, along for the ride to win extra credit points with the public.

All of the adults had been around long enough to see and hear the problems infecting our communities - but a lot of them just didn't want to deal with them anymore. They were burned out and jaded and had seen the system spit out the innovators. So it wasn't that they didn't know things were getting bad, they just didn't care. Co-founder Bailey describes the climate:

> Sometimes when I am introduced as a father of the political consulting profession, I wince. I don't blame myself for the shortcomings of our politics, but those of us who have practiced politics for the last forty years have truly made a mess of it.
>
> The consultants and ad-makers haven't done it alone. The quality of the candidate has gone down. The press has made every part of a public servant's life open to public scrutiny, driving good people from running for office. The need for money means only the rich and those willing to do expensive

favors are likely to run. And our TV culture has made a mockery of the whole process. But the most serious problem of all - more serious than the negative ads, the money, the cynicism - is that young people are so turned off to the system they run away from it. That means we become stagnant. And in time that means we die.

This is where we were: caught in stagnancy, amidst the hushed snickering in the Washingtonian circle of non-profit CEO's, public servants, White House correspondents, and political representatives. Every day, starry-eyed optimists spawn ideas into the civic arena and without fail, they all get snagged in red tape and bureaucracy.

Educators and government workers endure their nine-to-five cubicle-fest because they need a job. They have impressive titles with cushy benefits and are creatures of habit that don't want to be disturbed with new obligations. Professors aren't teaching because they are excited about shaping young minds; they're teaching because they have to meet a nine-hour lecture requirement in order to fund their research. Many of our own teachers don't even care. They walk into classrooms and sit at their desks and recite from a textbook. With jobs shutting down, they know that the state government is always going to have a mandate for primary education, so they teach. It's secure and it's bearable.

Our school employees are trapped in a Dilbert cartoon and for many teachers, education is regarded as just another day at the office. The employees sitting within cubicle cell walls aren't being asked to dream. Nobody cares if they are inspired by an idea or fundamentally believe in a cause. They're paid to increase the longevity of a system we've been stuck with for decades, a worn-out system that refuses to respond.

Too much of Washington politics follows this same trend. It is irrational. Republicans and Democrats slaughter each other just to win a game, with this unhealthy single-minded focus on victory. Politicians are the NFL Pro-Football players, so obsessed with gaining two yards that they don't even remember what's going on outside the stadium. They've battled up and down the field so many times, sloshed through the mud for so long, overused the playbook so much, that they've forgotten to look out to the stands and see that the fans are booing them. Or gone. We don't care about the game anymore. Americans want to go out onto their streets and see the problems solved.

Where's the Money?

Standing outside of the stadium, we realized that no one was going to toss us any free tickets. We had to force our way in and we couldn't do it with brute strength; we had to catch the ear of the owners. Before our five reps sitting as panelists at a Monday-morning press conference could multiply into a million kids from thousands of American high schools, Freedom's Answer would need to gain a legitimate reputation and secure funding. But we were enmeshed in this culture of false securities where the bold ideas are automatically written-off as impossible. Nobody wanted to tear down the cubicle walls and meet a kid-centered, un-tested idea on the other side.

Charitable foundations and donors didn't care about instinct. And with shrinking portfolios and quarterly lay-offs, companies were quick to send out their form letters with the resounding, "We are pleased that you consider us to be a community leader, but we are unable to fulfill your request for funding…" "We are sorry to decline your request for corporate sponsorship…" Proactive financial supporters of past Bailey and McCurry ventures even became skeptical, urging the pair to return to the drawing board and "maybe start off with a pilot program in some local community" and "see how it does".

The answer was NO. Freedom's Answer wouldn't compromise. We needed to see how far we could go. Why would we consider changing just a city when we could change a country? Something is seriously wrong when foundations are writing six-figure checks for studies to determine if two knocks or three is a more impressive way to get a potential voter to open the door - and refuse to give a few dollars to allow *students* to get into the *schools*. Trust funds are throwing away endowments to academics just so they can rewrite documents and make them less accessible to the mainstream public.

We don't need more talk. We don't need another "pilot program" working with ten kids who are dressed up and brought to the board meeting and then sent home. We need people who believe what they're saying. We're outside holding a rally, making something happen - begging the adults to disentangle themselves from public perception and paychecks and to invest in something sensational. The difference could not be more startling. They want to study the issue; we want to solve it.

But everyone rejected us, from the national corporations, down to our homey community hubs. The reluctance to lend us a buck was shocking. Tyler White, a cowboy-boot-wearing Texan, tried to win-over his grocery store only to leave with empty pockets.

> I've walked up and down those aisles forever. It was my hometown grocery store. I even recognized the pimply clerks there who were getting ready to go off to college. So of course, I thought it would be the perfect place to ask for support. The store was always giving money away.
>
> One day after school, I called and asked to speak with the manager. He listened to me as I explained what we were doing with Freedom's Answer, wished me the best of luck, apologized for not being able to be of any more help, and squirmed off to take another call. They had never heard of us before and didn't feel like taking a chance.

We continued to explore new leads, undeterred by large doses of pessimism. We learned to scrape the meat off the bones and worked harder to compensate for what we couldn't have. In the end, four major institutions along with individual donors served as our monetary contributors: AOL Time Warner (Co. and Foundation), the Knight Foundation, the Carnegie Corporation of New York, and Lockheed Martin. They gave us that first push on the swing, and we said thank you and did everything we could to keep pumping our legs.

Reputation Builders

We had six months to build a reputation, establish an infrastructure, and complete our mission - far too little time to generate complicated red tape of our own. At school, we don't set goals that are so vague that they become pointless. We don't tell ourselves that we want to "engage ourselves in competitive forums." We say that we're going to work our butts off to make Varsity. We're clear and we're straight with ourselves and we don't get lost in the semantics.

Most non-profit, youth-serving organizations have lofty mission statements. They mean well, they really want to do something - but they also want a job. If they achieve their mission, it means they're out of a job. And so they come up with these mission statements that could mean anything to anybody, that are unquantifiable and overwhelming. No one really knows what he or she is supposed to be doing because there isn't a tangible goal. Nurturing kids? Helping humanity? Sure that's noble, but how do you do that through internal publications and quarterly reports? This was our chance to finally take all the mumbo jumbo out of the memos and meet the masses face-to-face.

The first ears we caught were those of the non-profit ringleaders, contacts of Bailey and McCurry who had sway and usually, a multi-million dollar organization behind them. For a fighting chance to prove ourselves, we borrowed their names and their reputations to accrue legitimacy. America's Promise, a coalition of several hundred businesses, government agencies, and non-profits, the National Association of Secondary School Principals, and the American Bar Association had the rolodexes to get us into all the locked doors of corporate America. They were convinced that we were building something explosive and were the first to sign their names on a budding list of supporters. Peter Gallagher, CEO and President of America's Promise, expounds on his rationale for backing us:

> We believe the youth of this country represent the future and the fulfillment of our most cherished ideals: democracy, representative government, one

person, one vote. These are the ideals that must be embraced, nurtured, and protected by all citizens and certainly by our leaders of tomorrow. These principles must be embraced not just intellectually, but by action.

Those were the ideals articulated by Freedom's Answer, and the leadership was entrusted to America's newest generation - an army of students knocking on every door to get out the vote. Now it is their time, the young people who will lead us. Young adults, citizens with character and competence will be Freedom's Answer for America. This is what compelled me to be a founding member.

These were our visionaries - the movers and the shakers who ran from the dugouts to help because they fell in love with the idea. They gave us their direct lines, cell numbers and home email addresses and they meant what they said when they returned our calls. Kathy Bushkin and John Buckley at AOL Time Warner had the guts to write a check for a bunch of kids. Dr. Gerald Tirozzi, Executive Director of the National Association of Secondary School Principals, wrote letters to every American high school principal, and Peter Gallagher and Harris Wofford, from America's Promise, led our development meetings and pushed us to think big. Doug Pinkham helped us reach out to the members of the Public Affairs Council. We even had A.P. Carlton, President of the American Bar Association, setting up meetings and Jim Abbott, Director of Newspapers-in-Education, getting us space in print.

These scattered dreamers helped us catch the ear of the rest of the cynics. They provided that healthy dose of competition to their peers, forcing corporations and non-profits to think twice before completely ignoring us. And the peer pressure worked.

Names flooded down the advisory board roster as we welcomed responses from MTV, the National High School Coaches Association, and *U.S. News and World Report*. The Chairmen of the Republican and Democratic parties wrote a dramatic 4th of July op-ed in the *New York Daily News*. Even Congressional rivals co-signed joint Freedom's Answer letters. We had found a representative from every hue of American society: the educators, the government officials, the service organizations, the student leadership boards, national and local media, grassroots advocacy groups, web-based communities, and even internet providers. From the local pizza joints to the Statehouse, we wanted no one left out.

Although we may have been successful in our recruit in terms of quantity, many names were just that: names. Some "supporters" weren't diehard fans. They said "yes" because they had nothing to lose and because an "honorary" position doesn't take too much effort. But they didn't know who we were. When we called and asked for help, they asked us for our website address again, so they could "refresh themselves" about what exactly it was we were trying to do.

Nobody could argue that Freedom's Answer was pointless. It was definitely worthy - but so are a lot of other things. But a small minority was openly opposed to the idea and told us directly. Roger Ailes of Fox News Channel wrote, "I'm not sure freedom's answer is to go around and get a bunch of people to register to vote who won't do it on their own." Numerous others shared the doubts, but chose to keep them to the whispers. They may have given us their names, but they still doubted us. We had to prove ourselves to America.

The Young and the Old Reunited

Freedom's Answer wasn't an uptown million-dollar political convention with designer balloon elephants and donkeys. We were working out of some rented space in Washington D.C. and Denver and had a part-time, cut and paste network of grassroots staff, on loan to us from groups like the Center for Civic Education. Recruited state directors had makeshift offices that they decorated with home-made Freedom's Answer signs and personal outgoing voicemails that they rerecorded with a *Freedom's Answer* tilt. Stephen Johnson, a down-to-earth junior from New Jersey, explains:

> I called up our state director at his house to organize a 'Vote on the Mall' day and I heard the strangest voicemail: 'Hi! You've reached Cole Kleitsch, New Jersey State Assistant Director of Freedom's Answer. Feel free to leave a message - but you know what you've got to do. Vote 2002. We'll see you at the election.' I was stunned. It's great to see adults who actually care about what they are doing.

Their job was to help us out in the trenches, and some of them made the trek to see us and others didn't bother. Dealing with us is hard. We're supposed to lead the effort but we are sitting in chemistry class learning about organic compounds. We get out of school at the end of the day, trudge off to sports practice or band rehearsal, trailing a sixty-pound backpack spilling over with hieroglyphic-looking notes explaining how to find the cosine of a triangle - and then commute home and crash. Directors were slouching in their chairs and scratching their balding heads, trying to make sense of it. There was no way the schedules would intersect.

Shante Rawlings, a veteran of the youth service community, attests to the difficulties: "After sitting at a desk for twelve hours in front of a bottomless stack of papers, it becomes easy to 'forget' about the young people. We don't mean to leave them standing by the wayside, but there is no fast and painless way to work them into the daily routine." This time there was no good way to write us off. Freedom's Answer was centered on the results of a maturing generation and everything was riding on *us*.

The student-adult relationship broke the mold. Freedom's Answer Staff called us at school and left messages with our office secretaries. They flooded our cells with voicemails and started leaving the office progressively later, just to get in that extra half-hour and catch us decompressing on the sofa. We took more bathroom breaks at school and called back from the empty halls. We arranged 6:30 morning meetings and dashed off to school just in time to say the Pledge.

Why did our adult-student marriage succeed? The difference was that kids weren't asked to champion the happy, Rotary club monthly clean-up project. Kids organized and developed as partners alongside adults. It was more than just volunteering our time to band-aid the problems; it was finally yanking them out by the roots.

Matt Bales, a well-liked senior, describes the unprecedented structure of the organization:

> We're building a skyscraper. The corporations and associations are the pillars. They make the structure look sturdy. But they're just there to look good and loan us the weight of their name. They don't care

about what the blueprints are claiming or about the construction going on at the top. But that's good too, because they're busy having a nice chat with the building inspectors and letting us get to the real work.

We've got the hammers in our hands and are raising the roof on this thing. Bailey and McCurry, the architects, are gazing up at us, cheering us on through the radios. We're at 1500 ft! We stare at each other and then shout, "2000 ft!" Bailey's voice is crackling, "You're doing it. Keep going! Keep going!" We get to 2000. Again the rush... and then there's an echoing, "Hell, let's go 3000". This is the real deal.

All the other organizations were led and owned exclusively by adults with occasional youth afterthoughts, or they were college-based grassroots movements with almost no adult assistance. America lacked effective adult-youth mergers; the two groups had always tried to get along without each other. Even more compelling - America had never seen her *high school students* before; we were regarded as too young to offer anything serious.

So when the kids with the braces glued to their teeth, too young to sign a legal contract, stepped to the forefront - our visionary allies stepped to the sidelines to shout and wave banners like never before. And after a couple of laps, we understood just how valuable we were to each other. Most of our principals were sick of the kid fantasies and wanted to know why they should care, so we gave them the official letterheads. We took them to the website and made them scroll down the list of partners. We let them talk to any adult they wanted to but we never would accept, "no." Most of our superintendents, Board of Education members, and district supervisors were tired of adults and ached for a waft of our idealism.

Tess Reamer from Missouri, a diehard Keyettes officer describes the tradeoff.

> My advisor had been trying for days to get through to the superintendent's office, but nobody was returning her messages. Automatic recordings kept chiming back at her on every number. She called me and told me about her frustration, but said she was so happy that I had gotten the ten schools around our town to sign up. That weekend, an article about us was published in the local paper, and on Sunday night, I got a call. My mom yells up to me from the bottom of the stairs that a Dr. J. wants to talk to me. Bouncing down the stairs, I go through my mental registry. Dr. J. sounds familiar; I just can't remember where I've heard the name. I get on the phone and try to figure out who's on the other end. He says he's so glad to finally talk to me and that he can't wait to help us get to the rest of the schools in the district. Then he remarks on my great picture on the front page of the paper. Turns out Dr. Johnson is our superintendent.

We Emerge

Fundraising and crafting a reputation are important. Having influential supporters behind you and networks to use are essential. But even though they provide backing, they don't give breath to the dream. We needed our peers.

It's like that first lemonade stand that we wedged together with old cardboard boxes. Our dad was there cheering us on, loaning us a couple of dollars, taking us to the hardware store and maybe even watching us from the lawn chair as we scrawled our "gud leminade - 25¢"

posters in bright yellow paint. We were glad he was there, but we were even more glad that he wasn't doing it all for us. It made us feel proud; it made us feel like we were growing up. And when we were finished and ready to start selling our patented formulas, we wanted John from across the street to relish the moment with us. Even then, we knew that our best business partners were our own buddies.

Josh Lipsky, a seventeen year old from Maryland, with scruffy brackish hair and a look that screamed politician, was accustomed to the adult modus operandi of using kids to boost public relations. He didn't know that it could be any different. Like all of us, he thought that this was all they would ever let us do and we just had to suck it up and deal with it. But he saw an undertone that began to bubble to the surface, a possibility to finally bury the hypocrisy. Josh recounts:

> Freedom's what now? It's a voting drive? Non-partisan? And on and on the questions went until I was convinced this Freedom's Answer thing was legitimate. As we sat at that table in the mid-morning hours, we slowly began to grasp what Freedom's Answer was all about. How remarkable it was. An historic campaign that would dramatically change the face of youth activism, a campaign that would allow five kids to light a match with doubts and a million more to spread a bonfire with solid conviction. We had to start somewhere, we had to convince each other that we could do it… but no one could have ever imagined just how many frontiers we would conquer.

The mission was outlandish, but we could see it in our heads. It wasn't loaded with the jargon we're used to hearing about getting kids to "feel" important. They were important.

Our leadership was a conglomeration of fiery-eyed students from national youth boards. We had heard of the other organizations from floating applications in the career center or seen their logos at the bottom of a thirty-second public service announcement. But we had never had a conversation with other student leadership groups, much less worked together with them on a national project. So why would we do it? Why would we agree to work with complete strangers, just because someone asked us to?

Despite the fact that our organizations were vying with each other for grant money to push forward slightly different programs, we all shared a common disappointment with the role we were offered. Every one of us felt that stick jutting into our ribs as the "senior staff" had to whisper to their secretaries to remember our names. We were just constituents in another bureaucracy where action was irrelevant. We spend months on the phones proposing ideas, only to watch in disgust as each one is slowly butchered until it fits into their nice little package, in line with the office agenda.

We were all aching for a chance to be given free reign over an idea still in its infancy. Says Bryant Hall of the National Association of Student Councils, "We're tired of being called 'youth consultants' and 'liaisons' while our opinions are brushed aside. We are tired of posing idly at the table while others hold the influence. What if we had something to call our own?" Every one of us had witnessed adults dominate details and hand over the polished product. It killed us. We were sick of this. We wanted the problems, we wanted the challenge, we wanted to bite off so much more than we could chew and then pass it around in hallways. We wanted something meaningful to give each other.

That's why we stopped hesitating, overcame our reservations, and made a run for it. We may not have really understood what was happening but we got a whiff of what could be. Freedom's Answer was our organization to mold. Bailey and McCurry had made it explicit that this was no action figure they had given us to quietly play with in the corner. This was putty in our hands. The organization would develop either way - but we had to challenge the accepted standard and recognize that no one was imposing any limits to our partnership. Pointblank, we were asked to drive an organization forward.

Who is the "We"?

For the first indelible moment in history, we spoke to one another. Students from the National Association of Student Councils (NASC) Executive Board, Junior Statesmen of America (JSA), the Junior ROTC (JRROTC), and the Youth Partnership Team (YPT) of America's Promise got on our cell phones, driving home from weekend conferences and said, "So, yeah. We're going to do this!"

NASC's students represent a broad and potentially powerful constituency: student body officers, the kids who usually had a direct line to the principal. But who knew if the popular kid who was student body president would actually bother to help us pull this off. JSA were your typical political junkies, those kids who watch CNN and love it. To everyone else, they were just another face in the crowd, noticed only when they drove past in their cars plastered with campaign bumper stickers. But kids who *like* politics? Could average teenagers relate? JRROTC were the cadets whose national commander, Lt. General Timothy Maude, was killed at the Pentagon on 9-11. They walked around in military uniforms, were capable of running five miles after 100 pushups in a minute, and the community respected them. But no one knew if they could lead an army of their peers. The YPT were Colin Powell's kids - a national board of sixteen students well-bred in community advocacy, who had connections but no substantial student infrastructure. Together, we comprised the core of a still-expanding National Advisory Council of Freedom's Answer - The Idea Engine.

Our mandate was to figure out a way to talk to the rest of our generation. Freedom's Answer had endowed itself with an aspiration to smash the non-presidential voter-turnout record. The challenge was how to give our friends both something they could immediately buy into and something they wouldn't shrug off after a few days.

We mapped a strategy, deciding on three ideas that would form the heart of our program: (1) *Friday Night Football* - hanging out with our friends next to the concession stand - calling out to people to come and pledge their vote, (2) *Adopt a Block* - yelling across the street, "Miss Mary, remember we're picking you up tomorrow to cast 'yer ballot," as you walked through the neighborhood reminding eligible voters to cast their vote, and (3) *Take Ten* - calling our grandparents, our cousins, our aunts and uncles, for the first time in six months and asking them to pledge their vote to us. Leadership was in place. The message was being honed. Now to find the ground-troops.

The most obvious place to look was the summer conferences. Robbie Rader, a frizzy farm girl from Missouri, describes the sudden surge in membership. "The auditoriums reverberated with our presentations. You could hear the emotion swelling through the room, and then you were caught. A couple hundred students at a time, we spoke to a generation." The dream was infectious and we were intent on creating an epidemic. We had to ask the gatekeepers to let us in the door to talk - they did - and as we delivered our story, the sea of teenage strangers looked up at us with hunger in their eyes. The adults were less enthralled and made comments explaining how their board "doesn't really do anything except host meetings" and how they *"weren't in a position to try something new."* But the kids... they were floored by the idea, aching to explore new territory. New recruits were added to our databases and our National Advisory Council now housed leaders from Girls Nation, Boys Nation, the Hugh O'Brian Youth Leadership Program, YMCA Youth in Government, and the Boys & Girls Clubs of America.

The tight circle, which locked around us after a speech, questioned us relentlessly, wanting a way to follow. Their enthusiasm prompted the need for another, larger leadership board composed of *all* the energetic members from each of our organizations. We wanted to see what would happen when we combined the student council state presidents with the boys state senators and the kids from the 'Y' with the local 'cadets.' The thought was unfathomable! For years, national advisors had *talked* about making it happen, one massive forum where all the student leaders could finally speak to one another. They had discussed it and contemplated it, and perhaps the leaders of their associations even wrote up a memo. We called it the National

Leadership Council.

A Reason to Call

The National Advisory Council had to recruit the rest of the National Leadership Council, and it in turn would have to recruit every high school, and the student coordinators at each high school would have to recruit the entire student body. And it would be hard.

We knew the kids that we brought in from our own organizations, but we had no clue about the rest of them. On the weekly conference calls, we heard only voices and tried to connect subtle accents with names and places. Despite the fact that we didn't know if this guy was 100 pounds or a soaring 6'5", we knew that he cared. And that was enough. If this mystery kid bothered enough to get on the phone to do something, then we could spare the thirty minutes and listen. Tori Zoellner, an accomplished debater from South Dakota, describes the peculiarities of the situation:

> I was listening to all these people talking on the phone and it was like I was talking to ghosts. They were faceless voices sitting half way across the country and I kept trying to piece together what they might look like, but I always knew I was way off. The girl could be a diva or a ditz. There was no way to know - and I think that's what kept us together as one united fist. We couldn't make any preconceptions.

Across the course of our lives, we had met fascinating people through conferences or meetings or weekend sports events. We had hugged them and promised that we would stay in touch and keep talking; but we didn't stay in touch, because it's hard to stay in touch. When we were with them, the conversations spilled over into the hours of the morning, but as soon as we sat down to email them, there was nothing to say. Now there was something we had to say.

With mounting confidence, we dusted off our databases and called every name, every number, emailing each faded address scrawled on the corners of wrinkled papers. We dug down deep and searched through the decaying scraps of program agendas buried in our rooms, smiling at lost memories and retrieving forgotten names. We found our motivation to connect with these people, a reason to do something together - across organizations, schools, neighborhoods, and even time zones. Bernard Holloway, burly but short, issued a booming call to action to his student council presidents:

> This can't be another token project that we paste at the end of our annual report. This has to be more than any report; this has to be more than any term. This is our chance to find the rest of them, our friends. We hang out at the movies and at the mall and we try to explain that they can do the exact same things we're doing, and their eyes just glaze over and they say, yeah, sure and walk away. Can you imagine what's going to happen when we give this to them, when we hand over a national project and say, it's yours, no strings attached. They're going to finally realize that there are no limits. There's nothing that can't be done. But you have to find every one of them. And you have to hand Freedom's Answer over. You owe it to the rest of our generation.

A Generation Found

People were attracted to our call because it wasn't branded with any sort of stereotype. It wasn't just for the popular kids or for the kids obsessed with Green Party. It was for every single student who sat in a high school like the rest of us. Every one of us knew what it felt like to walk through those halls and be stuffed into the cramped cafeterias. We all knew each other, but thought that we didn't.

With Freedom's Answer, we sat down in the same room and worked on the same thing. We forgot that we were from different clubs and stopped trying to compete with each other. The Honor Society kids were wallpapering flyers with the Class President while Drama Club filmed a morning announcement with the video techies. The walls between cliques were lowered ever so slightly and we started trusting each other.

Nationally, our organizational pride turned to generational pride. The National Advisory Council and National Leadership Council were now bound communities, held together by commitment to a dream that was rapidly becoming discernable. We introduced our own corporate model. We built our national coalition and asked every high school student we could find to sit on our Board of Directors. From across the plains of America we found our peers, with their own private stash of tricks. Gals in Renfro Valley were charging an admissions fare of one voter pledge to get into the Kentucky Fried Chicken Festival. Guys in San Francisco flyered Fisherman's Wharf. Each one of us knew what spoke loudest to our own communities. Joe McFarland, a skinny basketball player with freckles from ear to ear, was stunned. "We forgot about limiting ourselves to our existing contacts, and we called up the whole damn nation. Who knew there were kids living in Idaho?"

Our parents saw the strange area codes showing up on phone bills and gave us inquisitive smirks as Rachel from Indiana called Brad in New Jersey. Amy Bembnister, a laid-back Wisconsin Badger, describes the incredulity of the surprise.

> Seated in a dim hotel lobby, I gazed through the revolving doors at the flags flapping on their poles outside. I waited and wondered, watching cars go by. Three weeks ago, I'd e-mailed two people whose names I'd found under the Wisconsin section on the Freedom's Answer website. We'd cautiously introduced ourselves bit by bit through e-mail and started charting our plan. Yet, as I watched the door, I realized that daily e-mail has no face.
>
> I felt another rush of air as the doors turned. The two approached me; we shook hands and situated ourselves in a comfortable cluster of couches and chairs near the window, glancing up at each other with fresh smiles.
>
> Little did we know how much we would come to value one another in the months of media interviews and presentations ahead. Together, we would make or break Freedom's Answer in Wisconsin. The three of us, only names on a screen until we met in that dim hotel lobby, would learn to appreciate the help of strangers. The race had started, but none of us were alone. Our pack moved along in formation together, each of us taking turns cutting the wind.

Our student leadership emerged from its chrysalis, rubbing its eyes - not even aware that all this time we had been transforming from nominal students to national leaders. We knew we weren't the spokespeople anymore, but we weren't quite sure what we had become either. Clarity rushed in during the last summer weeks when we were handed over the deed to the conference calls. Every Thursday the twelve voices of the National Advisory Council would converge and formulate which footsteps we would need to stomp out that week on our path to November. Here's the beauty: the call was administered and attended unequivocally by students. We were the ones asking our peers to sign up a thousand more schools; we were the ones conjuring up plans for the next media blitz. The direction was *ours*, the planning was *ours*, the execution was *ours*.

The Fleet

Jumping into the company car, we buckle-up and start grinning while the executives of our organization point out the defrost button and show us how to signal lane changes. They teach us to park and are quickly summoned back to their leather chairs by personal assistants. Hesitantly, they depart. A few quick words of advice and a jaunt around the parking lot have been the extent of our lesson, and *"now they're taking the company car out on the road?"* Keys are hesitantly placed in our outstretched palms and we are ordered to "keep it under thirty and stay off the highways."

We get through a dozen red lights and make it to Bailey and McCurry, who smile at the door and tell us to go back out and bring our friends. Cruising around, we notice jaws dropping as we coast past our friends. They've seen the company car before, but they've never seen a kid driving it. And if we could drive, then why couldn't they? So our generation grabs the keys to the old Chevy in driver's ed, scribbles a quick note for the principal, and follows us. This time we get on the interstate and figure we can push this thing to ninety.

Arriving, we turn off the engines, crack open the doors and look around. There are hundreds of cars lined up haphazardly in a once barren parking lot. Thousands of kids are waiting. Bailey and McCurry show us to an underground garage, leaving us in the midst of a shining fleet of SUV's, sports cars, minivans, eighteen-wheeler trucks, and sedans. There's a new company slogan painted on the sides: *It's yours.* We begin to adjust the mirrors, and feel the shape of a wheel that could take us anywhere. In the glovebox is a user's manual with the pages ripped out and a sticky note that says, "We mean it! *It's yours.*" There's a cell phone with the conference call number programmed into the directory and a map of America. We're supposed to find the rest of the country. They tell us to get there as fast as possible and that bumps and scratches on the new paint are part of the process. So we leave.

Is Anybody Listening?

Chapter 3

We had to get the word out. Across the hallway. Across town... the state... the country. All the way to the White House. But how?

It was September. Both adults and students were coping with the start of the new school year. There was no glamour of pre-election articles, no school-wide spotlight on the November election. Still, we *did* find students ready for another obligation and adults willing to spend another hour to help. And we *did* convince our principals to approve our plan to involve the entire school in Freedom's Answer.

We had always wanted to call the shots. But with student-ownership came student responsibility. What we learned was that 95% of real leadership happens backstage. It's more than press conferences and glamour; it's fighting a mainstream culture that tells you you're going to fail. It's hard work. And it takes guts not to give up.

We took our dangling student skeleton, gave it some structure, and put it to work. Roll-call on the National Advisory Council, the top working group of students, included twelve representatives: Brad Johnson and Corey Mock - *Boy's Nation*, Chris Schoen - *YMCA*, David Boyd - *Boys & Girls Clubs,* Henry Royce - *Hugh O' Brian Youth Leadership*, Josh Lipsky - *Junior Statesmen of America*, Khandi Johnson - *Junior ROTC*, Puneet Gambhir -

America's Promise, Victoria Zoellner and Allie Senger - *Girl's Nation*, Zach Clayton - *National Association of Student Councils*, and Tommy Preston, a South Carolinian who was a little bit of everything - *Student Council, Boys Nation, and YMCA.*

Charismatic, bushy-haired Zach, Chairman of the National Association of Student Councils, led the National Advisory Council. In turn, the Council led the ranks of our 250 member National Leadership Council of state representatives and national leaders from the same organizations.

It may have been the most high-powered group of American high school students ever convened. And we made good use of it. *Everyone* was invited to the forefront. Freedom's Answer didn't have a "student executive board" or special perks. Our formula was simpler than pre-algebra: if you worked hard and produced results, you were called on to do more. Getting the job done wasn't always glamorous. "All the leadership lived on the edge," Zach would say. "School is almost a full-time job, then we added *this* on top of it?" Insane.

Every Sunday night, 7:30pm EST, Zach opened the conference call of the 200+ National Leadership Council armed with an agenda and weekly priorities revolving around a theme like "a hundred local headlines by Sunday" or "contact 250 more schools." For twenty-five minutes, the National Advisory Council members shepherded the rest through marching orders - and then the line freed up for advice, encouragement, warnings, stories of success and frustration - even the inevitable barking of a dog no one ever admitted to owning. For an hour and half, America's busiest teens waited for the open mike to offer their own do's and don'ts.

Each week was a new affirmation that we were part of something bigger than our schools, our cities, and ourselves. We were interconnected - each one's fears lost in the inspiration of another's dreams.

Word of Mouth

Simple phone communication was often the easiest way to convince both skeptical principals and students that Freedom's Answer was worth their time and energy. Every week we worked the phones, spending thirty minutes chatting up a principal or an hour talking to an on-the-fence JRROTC Cadet. We started small campfires in every state, desperately seeking both quality and quantity. Struggling to convince disbelievers to *care* was always tough, sometimes disillusioning, but we stayed at it.

Some days, Zach checked-in with over seventy members of the NLC by phone. "I'd start at 5pm eastern time and end at 10pm west coast time. It was eight straight hours of calling." Staring at a flat-screen computer in his makeshift workroom, he disturbed more family dinners in a week than any telemarketer could have hoped, but persistence paid off. With the help of Dane Anderson and Lindsay Ullman, these three student council musketeers started a national phone tree that never stopped ringing.

Jittery cold calls quickly became comfortable with practice. But there were other means of connecting. Boys Nation Senators, like Brad Johnson and Cory Mock, spoke to their local American Legions, lobbying directors for access to student databases. Puneet Gambhir, a rising America's Promise star, battled faceless listservs trying to grab the attention of the American kid. And Tyler White of Texas's Junior State of America chapter faxed seven page packets to over 2000 schools in his state.

> I grew to hate the gray fax buttons and late nights jabbing in nine-digit numbers, but we were recruiting tens of thousands of high school students to participate in Freedom's Answer each week. Definitely worth a few numb fingers.

Jonathan Friedman relied on the infrastructure of his Tennessee Association of Student Councils (TASC).

> After exchanging ideas with Freedom's Answer NLC members from around the nation, I understood what we had to do. First, my team sent mail-outs to every member school in TASC. I knew the personal contact and the written information would be invaluable in encouraging skeptical schools to join. Next, at each of TASC's six regional leadership workshops, we presented a "how-to" for Freedom's Answer, drawing in nearly three thousand young leaders from around the state. Finally, we developed statewide call-a-thons.

California's Stacy Edgar lugged 10,000 flyers to various student conferences, passing them out in high school gyms and aging cafeterias. And five foot, six-inch Charlie Pollack drove across New Hampshire.

> It's funny how some things just seem to fall into place. The New Hampshire Association of Student Councils Executive Board traveled all over the state, touring high schools and towns promoting the project. We appeared on local and state television and crowded the radio airwaves with our story. The state newspapers all published articles as the word of the project quickly spread. The Secretary of State called to let us know he wanted to help… it

got bigger than I could have ever imagined.

Chris Schoen, a YMCA Youth and Government Governor, worked locally. "Just calling the schools in your athletic conference and asking them to participate could mean five more participating schools. Plus, if you already had a rival school, why not challenge them to a voter turnout duel?" Diane Payne, a North Carolina principal, was taken aback when she went to a football game at the opponent's Leesville High School and was asked to pledge to vote by the other team's students. "Wow!"

The words of our teachers, mentors, and parents appeared in our heads time and time again: You never get anything without working for it. As we toiled over the fax machine and memorized far-off telephone area codes, we laid the foundation for a new fortress in modern politics.

Surfing the Web

We had a secret weapon no national youth movement in the 60s, 70s, 80s, or even early 90s ever had before. The Internet. The September 11 Generation was the first age group that had the technology available to centralize all our operations on the web. Email and Internet access were widespread, cheap, and instant - three essential requirements for anything this fast moving.

To keep the NLC in touch, Puneet Gambhir suggested we brainstorm through a common listserv. Had a great idea, something that had worked on another project before? Bring it on. Brooke Davis, who was a "once a week" email checker said:

> E-mail was the best thing we ever could have hoped for. Had we all tried to write or phone one another,

we never would have had enough time. From my $900 Mac, I knew exactly what people were doing on every side of the country. And since we had only a few months, the instant connections we could make were priceless. Our state team contacted each other via e-mail at least once or twice a day or more for months.

Our chief tool was www.freedomsanswer.net, an interactive website that included brochures, letters, press releases, pledge cards, Take Ten forms, and instructions for all the programs of Freedom's Answer. With fifty thousand hits a day, we knew kids across the country were checking us out - they were also downloading flyers and powerpoints. When we brought on board another school, they signed up on the website.

The site was more than home base; it was an unparalleled resource for snagging recruits. But it went beyond linking us together and providing information. It reminded us why we worked so hard. As Jill Husman, a Senate Page in Washington, wrote:

> I was blown away by the flash intro to the website. It had pictures of firemen, soldiers, and ordinary people, it memorialized that second moment of 9-11 - a poignant combination of music and images that reminded us why declaring to the world with our votes that freedom was alive was so important.

The site showcased kids who were "heroes of the week," an honor awarded for extraordinary efforts, it offered message boards to post urgent ideas, it was an emotional e-hub.

NLC members also had their own extranet site with its unique pass-code. It was packed with sample op-eds, "how-to" pages, and letters to the editor. To avoid unnecessary duplication we posted common press releases and speeches. It allowed us to communicate a unified message instead of re-creating our own new witty one-liners. We could also check on which schools were signed up, who their kids were, and how many pledges they had recorded.

Valuable links from local and national newspapers, MSN, Yahoo!, PBS, Youth Noise, LEAP Kids, Do Something, SHiNE, and Kids Vote USA helped direct kids on the web to our site. FASTWEB emailed two million of our peers with an invitation to join us signed by our National Advisory Council. AOL bannered us on their internet radio stations, gave us a keyword, and hosted an online Freedom's Answer Forum with Senators Dodd and Bennett. The goal was friendly bombardment.

Convincing Adults that We Mattered

Our partnerships with adults in our states formed a valuable confederacy. We provided vigor; they provided infrastructure. Local American Bar Association lawyers heeded ABA President A.P. Carlton's call for support. With the help of the National Conference of State Legislatures, we asked state legislators to call their districts' principals.

Of course, we still personally lobbied our principals for the required sign-off on the website. Alicia Raia of New Jersey had a story that seemed like many of ours: "Initially, our principal didn't want to be bothered, didn't think it would benefit our school, and didn't think it was worth the output of time, resources, and energy." But Alicia forged forward. "The unabashed persistence of a group of students cannot be met with cynicism forever. We just simply wouldn't take 'no' for an answer." Her group "pleasantly" pleaded the cause, "We had been called to, not by merit of grades, recognition, or glory, but by simple call of patriotic duty." Hasty dismissals were changed into consideration, then participation.

It took JSA's Rob Santiago twenty minutes before he and his blue North Face book bag got the okay - complete with a pizza party promised to the top homeroom. Others who encountered more difficulties made use of the adult-to-adult intervention Freedom's Answer State Directors could provide. It even took one of our top National Advisory Council members months to convince her local principal to sign-off. When denied, there was only one real option. Fight back. In time, most of us won out. It's amazing how adults become less obstinate if you bother them enough.

One alternate route we used to jump roadblocks was involving state officials. Governors signed proclamations declaring "Freedom's Answer Days" and state legislators were hit up for their support and political capital to influence schools in their districts to sign up for Freedom's Answer. Bernard Holloway field-tripped to Annapolis, Maryland to personalize the drive behind the program:

> State capitols are frequently packed with individuals lobbying for bills, protesting legislative action, and asking for support for many different organizations. Amidst this zoo of activists, Freedom's Answer emerged as a priority for many state legislators. We were no-frills advocates, tentatively walking door to door into the offices of state senators and representatives to distribute information about Freedom's Answer.

Most of us asked legislators to contact schools in their districts and urge them to sign up. They helped assuage dubious principals' qualms. Principal wouldn't listen? Nothing a conference call with the state senator couldn't solve. Many legislators also volunteered to speak at local high schools about the importance of voting. Pennsylvania's Tom Brown was both booed and lauded at his State Capitol:

> You would think that many legislators would be unreceptive to spending time helping a non-voting student. In some cases, that was true. I walked into one legislator's office midday to give my normal description of Freedom's Answer and what it was trying to accomplish. I was "greeted" by a secretary blankly staring at her computer screen, speaking to me in a low, disinterested voice while I tried to explain this organization, this movement that meant so much to me. (She didn't take her eyes off the screen once until I left.)
>
> But as we went from office to office at the Capitol Building in Harrisburg, the openness and support of the vast majority of House members astonished me. We were actually able to obtain meetings with many of them - a half-hour talk with my representative, soda with one representative from Malvern. Almost all agreed to support the program by sending letters out to high schools in their districts encouraging them to sign up for the program. But I think just as importantly, we sent a message that the youth of America are not intemperate and ignorant of the political process. Rather, they can be the driving force behind revitalizing our system of government.

A few days after his trek around Harrisburg, Tom Brown checked the Freedom's Answer website and was pleasantly stunned. "In a matter of days, Pennsylvania had doubled its total from three weeks before - and I saw the names of schools in the heart of the legislative districts of representatives we had spoken to."

Media

We didn't want to just reach principals and students, we wanted to inundate them. As "the Boss" of every high school reclined in her overstuffed principal chair to check out the Metro Section, we wanted heartening stories about high schools in her face. We needed her to want to be one of those schools in print. We wanted peers to see their lab partners on page A1 and be inspired.

Big national pieces squarely confirmed how widespread our efforts were while local coverage profiled students with riveting stories that caught community attention. Principals were delighted they could put a national newspaper clipping on the bulletin board and boast to their colleagues that their school was part of this nationally acclaimed "civics program."

How valuable did the program seem once it showed up in the local paper? Freckled junior John Schiltz: "It seemed like a cool idea, but I didn't think the program was anything more than our student council president's pet project. Then our newspaper profiled the school, mentioning that thousands of other schools were doing the same." Robert Wrallings of Oklahoma said, "Local coverage convinced our moms and dads that all those late-nights were worthwhile." It showed how real a national program was to small communities.

The Newspapers in Education program of the

Newspaper Association of America undertook a partnership with us, the first time they had ever endorsed an outside idea. They set a goal of having five hundred of their papers feature Freedom's Answer in special inserts. But still, much of the local coverage came from dogged calling to newspapers and begging them to check out a great story. We all had access to press packets online, including sample press releases, and anyone could look up media contact information. Indiana's Heather Bostich took advantage of that to mail 100 press releases. Though she was frustrated to "use so many stamps up," and only receive three or four responses, she said, "The radio show and two articles were worth it. They added huge momentum for us."

Not only is all politics local, all local media is really local. Mike, the dreamy WXYZ reporter, just isn't a hotshot two towns over, in WEFG territory. So when we called kids a few hundred miles away to beg them to sign their school up, we needed something a little more widespread. National coverage gave us substance and touched millions.

Sunday, September 8, *Parade* (circulation: 34 million households) kicked off our effort for the September 11 anniversary week with a Freedom's Answer feature by David Oliver Relin. On Monday, students were knocking on their principal's doors, waving the article, and convincing him or her that our idea wasn't some hare-brained student scheme. Respected columnists like Al Hunt of the *Wall Street Journal* and Marty Schram of *Scripps-Howard News Service* wrote profiles on our leadership. Allison Jones of *The New York Times* gushed when she heard our stories, and publishers like Orange Quarles of the Raleigh *News and Observer* made sure stories appeared in the

Sunday paper. Many papers, like the *Denver Post*, ran Freedom's Answer editorials. Stacy Edgar schmoozed talk-show hosts on Fox, Allie Senger appeared on CNN's *Inside Politics*, and Zach Clayton argued with Nachman on MSNBC.

Reporter Meredith Meyer of the Sioux Falls *Argus Leader* reacted in a way we saw often: "The average daily news report includes information about kids jacking cars, having sex, and doing drugs.... These young people were working toward something they were passionate about - and neither work ethic nor empathy is common among your average teenager. It was refreshing to report the good being done by kids instead of the bad."

Each story written, and every nightly news broadcast aired for Freedom's Answer allowed more people and more schools to hear about our program. Friends slapped us five with "Hey, saw you on the News last night," and principals beamed. The news made us authentic.

America's TV culture may ridicule politics, but TV was our best friend. Powerful moving images of kids in flag-filled gyms meeting Congressmen, rallying around Freedom's Answer, played perfectly on camera. The American Bar Association pre-recorded a Video News Release and mailed it to every TV station in the country. But Oregon's Dylan Ordonez went even further:

> I wondered how I could take advantage of the tele-vision in my small community. We had already flooded the town with flyers, articles in the paper, and other ways of getting the word out, but I want-ed to take it to the next level. I talked with my superintendent about using the local television to air a student-produced, non-partisan commercial sim-

ply urging people to take advantage of their right to vote.

The cable company had given us a rough estimate about how much it cost to buy ads, which our student group deemed reasonable, so we voted and allocated $1,000 for the project to put our ad on the air. Once we notified the cable company of our idea, they were blown away. Instead of just airing the number of ads our dollars would have bought - they aired one thousand ads with our $1000! 1,000 times for our $1,000 dollars on 12 stations for the two weeks before the election. It was a blessing.

Our cable company only extended across portions of 2 counties in Oregon. So we didn't expect to reach more than maybe 25K-30K people. But some of the major news stations up in Portland heard about our project and decided to do a report on it. We were featured on the evening news, which went across the entire state. Oregonians heard about our small town's efforts to get citizens to vote, the most crucial element in our democracy and we got more publicity from $1000 than many candidates did with their whole budget! When Election Day came, we knew that we had done what we could to help make our country a better place.

We made it through the month and finally realized there was no place left to look but up.

The White House

Landing on the runway at Reagan National Airport, catching the Amtrak down to Union Station, or dashing through the Metro trains into Foggy Bottom - some seventy students of the National Leadership Council arrived in the city of "big-talk." Most of us had been in Washington before. We had seen the monuments of Jefferson and

Lincoln. We had even taken a tour of the White House and had strolled around the Capitol building. But this time we came as more than bystanders. We weren't here to be told again why things hadn't changed; we were here to launch the change.

Gathered in a hotel courtyard, faceless names suddenly appeared before us in navy suits and dresses with red, white, and blue lapel pins. The hours we spent on the phone with each other flashed through our minds, and we just smiled and shook hands. On scraps of yellow-lined paper, we coordinated who would say what and attempted a dry run of our press conference before boarding buses to the Dirksen Senate Office Building. Amanda Cullen, a late night workaholic, reflected:

> I live in a suburb of DC, so I'm pretty used to the city. It's like home. But when I saw these people, a few who had never even been on a plane before, get so excited, I couldn't help myself. It was like I saw Washington for what it could be - a place that would welcome not just one busload of dreamers, but a place where a hundred buses could bring floods of students. We always look back on history and events like the Civil Rights movement and the Labor Movement. Who said this can't happen for every group of people who believe enough? We were going to our government leaders to ask them to get on board. They had the choice, to decide whether they were going to help us now or after the rest of the country got behind us. It was our turn to ask.

While stalled at the security checks on Capitol Hill, we hurriedly matched almost one hundred faces with names, scanned the cramped corridors and reintroduced ourselves to those around us. Clamoring out of elevators into the halls of the sixth floor, we had a second round of hand-shakes with the adult leadership of Freedom's Answer who stood guard outside our pressroom. Our pressroom. Behind the podium: a stunning map of the United States of America in red, white, and blue - each state bursting with stars that symbolized registered Freedom's Answer high schools. It was a map of a student nation aching for a chance to redefine "citizen."

Local media fought for floor space in the back of the room, while the larger national broadcasting companies already had cameramen staking-out their reserved spots, dead center. There was barely enough room for us all. Students spilled over from one side of the room to the other. Bailey got up to the podium from his seat in the audience and gave a quick introduction, remarking chiefly, "By no means is this my show to run. This is theirs," and exuberantly returned to his seat.

Puneet Gambhir recounts the scene:

> Then Zach got up. It was like for three months the guy had been just letting this thing smolder in his stomach. During his summer in Spain, instead of enjoying the foreign beaches, he was writing emails at internet cafes, trying to organize people to speak at summer conferences. And for Zach to get up in front of CNN and the other big shots…it was magical. When he talked about the million students knocking on doors in America, it was like he was watching this movie in his eyes and describing the scene to us. He could see it, and he gave it to all of us to see. He heard it, and he gave it to all of us to hear. The words didn't really matter. When you feel that kind of conviction in someone's voice, when you feel that kind of conviction in a *seventeen-year-old's* voice, chills run down your spine.

All twelve National Advisory Council students stood before blaring lights and colored the program for the audience. Each gave their own one sentence definition of Freedom's Answer: "14-15-16-17-year-olds standing and defending our nation and our rights the only way we can... a voice in our democracy and a way to show our patriotism... it's more than just politics now... a declaration against apathy... a chance for our generation to lead."

Zach summed it up: "Freedom's Answer is a record turnout caused by students too young to vote. When they say only in America, maybe that's what they mean."

After a pronounced silence, movement in the corner began to attract eyes. A scrolled parchment - sparkling white with a state-by-state listing of schools in red and blue - was unveiled. Students snaked it around the room's perimeter in a one hundred foot line beginning with Alabama and ending on Wyoming. Oregon's Dylan explained the building emotion:

> In two days, I had traveled more than 7,000 miles for over twenty hours, from one American coast to the other, but it was worth it. For the first time, after listening to telephone messages and watching the flash opening on the website, I finally got to see it live. I got to see our message, and our message was us. The whole group that had made the trek to DC was finally together in one room. And through the uncoiling scroll, we were handing a torch off to each other, looking at the person next to us, and saying, 'Here, this part is yours.'

But we still had to blow it over the top. Stacked on a table next to the podium was a thick pile of white poster sheets. Picking one up, Zach turned and revealed the front as low gasps fell through the aisles. The words "An American Declaration" stood at the forefront, while the Statue of Liberty and a dark New York skyline suffused the backdrop. And through a glittering city outline appeared the twin towers of blue light piercing the night sky. By name, we called each student to receive a declaration, signed by American Bar Association President A.P. Carlton.

For thirty seconds everyone stopped. In busy "go-go-go" Washington D.C., everyone stood still. Collecting whatever we had just given each other, we allowed the words to reverberate, we let the full weight of the meaning sink through, and we captured images in mental photo albums. Leading us by the hand, reporters rushed in and snatched their local hero off to some private corner for an interview. National correspondents selected the kids with the widest grins and asked them to say a few words for the camera. Congressional representatives shook our hands and discussed possibilities for further involvement. We rolled up the scroll, made our way to the elevators and left the podium empty.

From there we departed to the feted AFL-CIO office building for sandwiches and chips. We had given the media enough for the day, now we just had to find the White House. Our confidence was contagious and we spent more time learning stories and meeting new kids who apparently had passed through our hometown airport or heard of our girl's soccer team, all the while jotting down phone numbers for the weeks ahead.

Striding the two-blocks to 1600 Pennsylvania Avenue, our clusters mixed and we posed with each other in front of statues, asking strangers to stop and take our pictures.

Often times, the excitement even spread to them, and the passerby would crouch down on a knee, motioning with his hand, "a little to the left, okay, now you, you in the black-striped suit, you go to the back." A buoyant Erica Minor: "I just hope that everyone can at some point in their lives be a part of something this big. It teaches you how important one can be. And it teaches you how important one million can be."

The Old Executive Office Building of the White House loomed in front of us. We popped mints in our mouths as we passed through security, focusing ourselves. Pictures of presidents from Washington to Bush lined the walls. We admired the décor while climbing up the spiraling marble steps, but we weren't drooling over the expensive sculptures, we were reminding ourselves of the hundred kids back home who couldn't come. We were reminding ourselves of a nation of kids who didn't know they could come. Bernard Holloway, an effusive senior from Maryland, describes the event:

> All of us piled into the corridor, leaning against the cool limestone walls, trying our hardest to keep out of peoples' way. A sense of expectancy came over many of us. We were in the White House. The mood was escalating because we had nothing else to do but wait and hear the message again in our heads: We were in the White House. More concentrated, we engaged in conversations but weren't really in them. We continuously watched the door with sharp eyes, hoping to recognize a face among the herds of fast-moving Executive Assistants who darted around, but gave up as they rushed on by to the next meeting. Peering at watches, we let another hour slip by; we heard rumors that a briefing on the President's health was running over in the room

we were supposed to use. Getting restless and fidgeting with ties and high heels, we stared at the closed doors. Finally, one set opened. Out streamed some fifty or so stately figures - striding off down the corridor never once looking back to see a crowd of eager kids. They wouldn't look now, but we would make them look later. We filed into the room, took our seats in the plush chairs and waited.

After some minutes, a White House staff member broke away from a tight circle of adults at the front of the room and walked to the podium. Speech in hand, a representative of the White House Political Director explained the President's priorities in preparation for the election with a standard twenty-minute spiel. We listened patiently, reflecting on our own eleventh-hour operation. Glad to be done, he retreated to the audience, and another face went up to the podium. This guy was quite animated; he had taken off his jacket somewhere, and had rolled up his white cuffs, giving him the appearance of a skinny minister ready to stir something up. Shifting from the balls of his toes back to his heels, Ron Christie, Executive Assistant to the President for the USA Freedom Corps, looked out into our eyes, bit his lip and threw his papers on a chair behind him.

We all cracked smiles and listened intently as he tossed prepared remarks aside and decided to speak to us. "…America has not appropriately recognized the role its 'kids' should play in politics. America has ignored its newest generation." He genuinely continued, emanating a refreshing sincerity, "but it means so much more that in spite of incredible difficulty, you all have come on your own to deliver a message to this country - that America's youngest leaders will not be ignored… I congratulate you."

With his words still hanging in the air, we traded places. He took a seat in the audience and we treaded up front. With practice from our earlier press conference, the words fell more naturally and the pauses became more poignant. Every hesitation was calculated. We encircled the entire room with our scroll, students locked in a ring, holding their section of the testament with pride while adults rose from their seats and turned their heads from one side of the room to the other. They walked the circle, searching the names with hope that perhaps they would find their own high school - some did. Again, Washington D.C. listened to where the footsteps were falling across the rest of the country.

Letter in hand, we completed our request to the White House. Karen Edwards, a prim redhead from Ohio with bona fide flair, explained:

> We had asked to meet the President, hoping to deliver our message to our global representative directly. He himself was busy on the campaign trail. We understood. But we refused to give up an opportunity to leave a mark in the midst of an onslaught of White House briefings. We handed a letter to Ron Christie that we asked him to present to President Bush. It was a letter describing to him our mission, our commitment, and our vision. We asked Bush to ask Martin Sheen - U.S. President on NBC's The West Wing - to help us cut a public service announcement for high-level broadcasting on the network in the weeks before the election. An outlandish request, maybe, but why not? We were all about the impossibilities.

Ron Christie looked at the envelope, looked back at our faces, and pocketed the letter, nodding his head in slow, defining jerks. Out of the back of the room, another voice sounded - Mary Matalin, the Senior Advisor to the Vice President. The in-vogue chief had been watching us quietly from the back of the room. Marching forward, even before the twelve National Advisory Council reps had a chance to sit back down, she climbed up on the platform and started talking. She was mesmerized by what we had just done and told us so. Cracking jokes about her husband, CNN's James Carville, and how the black Ron Christie was really her adopted son, she spoke about the power of our dream. We couldn't have hoped for anything better.

As Mary Matalin ended with a fiery, "good luck" and "Godspeed," seventy teenagers migrated toward Mary and Ron to shake hands and snap photos to pass around back at home. Eventually, *all* of us teetered on the low stage, holding on to each other through a four-minute photo session.

The astonishment was mutual. We were thrilled to brief them on our activities, and they were equally inspired by our vigor and determination. Commenting on the exchange, Ron Christie wrote in an email, "As Mary and I walked back to our offices, we were simply stunned at what these students have done." We had allies at the White House.

Back on the bus, we sat down, leaning deep into the headrests, and saw a country where every student in America could stand with us. Headed back up Constitution Avenue for round two, we jumped off buses for a final expedition to the House and Senate buildings. Armed with flyers and info packets, we dropped by our Congressional offices.

Finally, ready to call it a day, our clusters tried to regroup. But the rain began to pelt the ground and the street where the buses were scheduled to pick us up was blocked for security. Most of us found, or were found by, the bus, the rest of us took metros and cabs back to the hotel - wandering at random intervals into a deserted lobby to grab luggage and catch flights or trains back to our nook of America. There wasn't any real closure to our day, no chance to hug goodbye or to promise to call the next night. We all just left.

But our goodbyes wouldn't have meant anything anyway because leaving was far from any goodbye. During the hours we spent traveling home again, we mulled over the words and images of the last twenty-four hours. *When you leave here today, you are going to go back home with a purpose...* We knew teammates across the country were counting on us. They were faces now. There was an Amanda and a Dylan and a Puneet somewhere out there just waiting for us to send that late-night email.

After meeting with the White House, our principal seemed a little less powerful. Our schoolwork seemed a little less pressing. That physics problem-set didn't have the same urgency. But there was still a void in the voice of America - ours.

Hometown Touchdown

Chapter 4

Thomas Jefferson High, East Central Senior, New River Upper - this is where we live. Every day for the last decade, we have walked through the double doors of America's high schools only to be lectured on expectations. Before, we swallowed it, allowing ourselves to be molded into cookie-cutter students, but now we were desperate for a higher purpose, a better reason to get out of bed at the blare of an alarm.

There had to be something more than mechanical busy-work, constant testing, and an assembly line education. We wanted an answer. Our minds, checking every angle, every outlet, finally forced us to look up - into the eyes of a hungry generation. We had to show them what they were missing.

After conversations at the Capitol and promises at the White House, we were back on home turf. The dreaming had infused us with urgency and a dire sense of "now" that made us scramble back to the congested hallways to challenge our peers. They gave faces to our million-kid movement. They were the reality of our vision. But we didn't have them - yet. We had to construct a bridge between the dreamers and the doers. Rhetoric had to become clear and attainable action steps. Searching for a model, we looked in our back pocket and relied on an adaptation of the formula we had used to expand nationally. Now we just had to break apart big ideas into a checklist everyone could digest:

- ✔ Form a core leadership group.
- ✔ Earn credibility.
- ✔ Expand your base.
- ✔ Execute a plan.
- ✔ Involve the community.
- ✔ Make a personal connection.

Six small steps for experienced leaders, six giant leaps for school kids. But hey, we were shooting for the moon.

Form a Core Group

Starting up a program in the midst of a hundred other ongoing programs is daunting. Faculty, already over-worked, don't want to have to deal with 'another' agenda item - so they run kids through the gauntlet, put up a list of demands, and hope the idea gets killed. One person can't effectively lead a movement or push an idea because it's easy to silence one person. But twenty kids standing together outside the principal's office forces others to pay attention.

Tracking mud in from the soccer fields, dashing from dress rehearsal still wiping off stage makeup, or stopping by after sitting around with a bunch of friends and a guitar - they came. Rarely would this crowd ever voluntarily meet up for an afternoon brainstorming session; it was a group of complementing personalities involved in different activities. They weren't necessarily the golden boys and girls of high school, but they were respected, had access to the ears of their peers and the influence to carry the project forward.

If we were actually going to attempt to engage our entire student body, there was only one way to make it happen. One student, that single kid completely sold on Freedom's Answer, would have to organize a gathering of leaders and convince them to collaborate. And it's not like people haven't sat down and tried to do this before. For semesters, teachers or students "have seen the real need for cross-club interaction." They had even arranged the lunch meetings, and still nothing happens. How would this be any different?

This was something huge - that realistically required the skills of an entire spectrum of leadership. We had always wanted to work together, and here, finally, was a way to do it without stepping on each other's toes. There was enough for everyone to sink their teeth into something.

Katie Sciortino of St. Scholastica Academy amassed her dream team at a lunch meeting. "Some were already visible leaders, others had the desire to lead," she explained. "Most barely had time to go to bed at night or the energy to jump in the car and make it to school in time. But they were willing to try this for one reason: it was finally a way for us to connect." This was uncharted territory. There were no legacies to fulfill, no obligations to tradition, no expectations to live up to. Ricky Perez of Maine addressed the "Dream Team" this way:

> We all finally made it to the same meeting! We're all here! How crazy is that. I know you asked me about the difficulty the SU [student union] had in setting up one of these shindigs, because no one ever shows up. Nobody showed their face because there was nothing worth working on - it was always

just for the sake of 'working on something *together*'. But let me tell you...this here is something sweet, because it demands us to use *everything* we've got.

Now we needed an avant-garde advisor. Especially in a school environment, there was no way around it. In order for us to be a "campus program" we would need a faculty advisor. So we just looked for the best. Someone who cared so much about young people that he or she allowed us to make mistakes, to slip and rise again. We needed that fiery guide who revived our hope when we looked at a multitude of lackadaisical adults and lost faith. They would be our number one fan, our advocate with the faculty, and a friend we could trust.

Jenny Lyons of Oklahoma describes the relief of finding that instrumental ally:

> Some kids wanted the lunch lady who always gave double scoops of ice cream on Friday or the robotics teacher who had a flag signed by the last six presidents. This one girl though, when I asked her, her eyes flashed and she softly said, 'What about Mr. Lopez.' Mr. Lopez was this comical seventy-two year old with a cane he used as a floor hockey stick. I walked past his door and saw him laughing with a ring of former students. Mr. Lopez. Why not? So I strolled inside, reintroduced myself, and twenty minutes later was sitting breathless on the other side of a desk thinking how lucky I was. This guy was awesome. Not only did he guide me into the answers - he taught me how to lead.

Organizers like Jenny pulled small coalitions together, plotting from obscure corner offices and the desolate lobby bench. The next step was to enlist the support of the adults who could add stature to the project. We could sell a cause to kids our own age, but we couldn't always expect the same result from other age brackets.

Have Credibility

The first question kids grill you with is, "Who are you?" They look for a reason to care, a reason to know that spending the next ten minutes of their lunch listening to you is a worthwhile investment. The even tougher sell is teachers who are so busy stressing about standardized testing and mid-year evaluations that they refuse to help you plug another program. We needed the "important" adults to help us get through all the start-up procedures. Their name beside ours would convince businesses to listen and teachers to lend class time. A required principal approval and buy-in from the community was necessary for our town to take us seriously.

The first time we solicited allies, hardly anyone let us get farther than "We need your help." Principals and teachers were overworked and too tired to listen; business leaders took one look at their already impressive list of "community initiatives" and pointed to the door. Even local youth-serving coalitions didn't understand why they should take some "airy kid-project" under their wing. They were already immersed in their agendas and didn't think we deserved their time. Responding to the frustrations of the thousands of students facing rejection, we circulated this email to every adult contact on file:

> 'There's not enough time' is the same as saying, 'I can't be bothered.' Time was short, but the firefighters dousing flames on 9/11 did not say that they 'couldn't be bothered' to do their duty. Time

was short but the servicemen shipped to Afghanistan to risk everything they had for freedom did not say they 'couldn't be bothered' to do their duty. Time is short, but no citizen asked to defend their greatest blessing of freedom - the vote - should say they 'can't be bothered' to do their duty and help reinvigorate democracy.

We never gave up. We knew if we got one behind us, another would come. So we persevered through rejections and kept battling to earn our credibility, enduring the sour experiences, and dusting ourselves off, even more determined to make people care.

The school was our core, so the most logical ally to enlist was our principal. Oftentimes the idea of a mass student-body campaign mesmerized administrators and they helped us run through the procedures of establishing a new school-wide program. In other districts, it was hard even to get them to pay attention. California's Stephen Howard, a drummer in his own garage-rock band, describes resilience.

> I was still the stranger sitting in the principal's office during lunch. Four years in high school and I had never been introduced to the 'woman in charge.' There just never had been a need to go and talk to her before. I mean, I wasn't the student body president or the 'It's Academic' semi-finalist. I'm a kid who likes video games and street hockey. The secretary came to the door, stuttering, trying to remember my name. 'It's Stephen, ma'am. Stephen Howard.' Nodding her head she apologized and said that something else had come up and Dr. Williams was canceling our meeting again. I got up, collected my Freedom's Answer folders, and walked out. Before leaving, I asked the secretary to deliver a message to Dr. Williams: 'Tell the princi-

pal I'll be back tomorrow.' If I had to herd up all my friends and spend every lunch in her office until she would make time to see me, then fine. I refused to get lost in the crowd.

We staged our own informal sit-ins, showing up every morning to check on the status of our request or calling every afternoon to leave another voicemail. These adults - our principals, our teachers, our community officials - had all stood on podiums and made promises to us once. Now we reminded them of their words and asked them to honor their position and to help us. After snagging the first couple of heavyweights, we felt the tension ease and saw the ears perk up when we told other adults who already supported us. An adult was at our side now, whether it was our principal or a respected staff member or even a PTA officer. They could give us legitimacy as we stood up and said we wanted students to rise and influence an entire community - young and old alike. Sarah Rodriguez, a 17-year old vocalist known for her choir solos, took a faculty meeting by surprise in her hometown of Helena, Montana:

> As I sauntered through the darkness, memorizing my speech, I tried to imagine the faces of the faculty smiling back at me. There would be Coach James, leaning back in his chair, trying not to fall back asleep, Mrs. Dalziel frantically taking notes to share at her next Social Studies forum, and even Mr. Moore, the physics chair who hated student projects and vehemently opposed 'new programming.' I strolled into the library and placed a Freedom's Answer packet on each of the sixty-two seats. Within minutes of the 'call to order' the rest of my partners in crime showed up, still pruning themselves. Introduced, we rose and blew the roof off the place.

Ditching all the memorized lines we stared each one of them in the eye and made them listen to us. They couldn't fiddle around with their agendas or pass whispers - because we weren't just making eye contact. We were challenging their preconceptions. Forty minutes later the swarms of crazed teachers engulfed us, and we shook hands and took down room numbers and home email addresses. Mr. Moore even waited in line to see me and remarked, 'Now Sarah, I do not believe in the meaningless programming that we promote at this school. But you know - this - this has some potential.' Yeah, I knew that.

It took guts to stand up in front of the entire faculty; it was hard to sway their set-in-stone opinions. They constantly remind us that they've been teaching here since the building went up in '79. But we found the right people to send in and do the job, and although it was tough even for them in the hot seat, they swallowed the lump in the back of their throat and got adjusted to the bright lights.

Having established a reputation within our own school, we cast our eyes to the bustling centers of activity in our community and extended our network of support. Students left campus, drove to the local Starbucks and asked the managers to host our nightly strategy meetings. We went to Blockbuster and established a student incentive program: "one free rental, every fifty votes." We even dressed up and went to offices downtown to invite the local government officials and lawyers to come back with us and inspire our assembled student army. Waqas Farid, an intense student councilor with killer speaking skills, narrates one unusual afternoon in history class:

Striding into the classroom, the three-piece suited

lawyers stood in front of a history class, not sure where to start or even what to say. Quickly reviewing the Edison High Freedom's Answer program, I looked to our impromptu panelists and asked them why democracy and freedom and civic liberties were something high school students should care about. Those words touched off a firestorm. They were taken aback. It stung to think that such a fundamental argument had gone untouched outside the monotonous history lessons. With passionate dynamism they spoke, often interrupting each other mid-sentence with another compelling burst of argument. Students could have tried to deliver the same oration to each other, but it wouldn't have had the same impact. Well-versed community leaders affirming our beliefs compelled us to start the fight for an active citizenship. Well-versed community leaders, honestly defending deep-rooted ideals, compelled them to pick up the fight with us.

Freedom's Answer was no longer just the project of a couple of kids in homeroom. We had formed the pyramid structure that would allow us to generate momentum and execute a widespread call to action. If the rubber was going to hit the road anywhere, it had to be at home.

Expand Your Base

Christened "legitimate" by their principals, school leadership teams handed Freedom's Answer over and asked that the rest of our generation move to the forefront where they belonged. The fiery and the passionate, the reserved and the timid; all kinds of kids banded together in our school-wide expansion. This is when we made our buck count, and reminded our leadership of the hundred kids they had standing, waiting behind them.

After all, even MLK Jr. couldn't end segregation alone. Our leadership group had to develop a powerful assembly to resonate with every club and clique - the microcosms that make up high school. If 20 kids could impact a community, then 500 or 1,000 could conquer it. We had to find the direct links to our peers and a message that made our call relevant.

We scoured for opportunities to make the five hundred, the thousand, the two thousand kids consuming our courtyards and our classrooms care. We stormed existing clubs and we combed the hallways, searching faces for imagination, energy, and desire. On the field, the ferocity of our classmates' competitiveness astounded us; their inventiveness in art class was ingenious. Now if only our peers would use their voices to call upon voters with the same intensity.

There was an element of risk. It was intimidating to ask peers to do something for us. But what if Columbus had been bashful about asking for three ships? What if Rosa Parks had been shy about her dissatisfaction with the Montgomery City Bus Company?

When her state student council organization chose Freedom's Answer as its annual service project, Emily Spence, a rodeo-loving, bull-riding Tennessean was convinced this was a wake-up call to her inactive student government:

> I stood up before ninety-eight members of the Central High student council. Today, I would be asking them to cast their own votes, asking them to vote to make Freedom's Answer ours. I knew that if they chose to do it, the rest of our students leaning against their lockers, wouldn't be far behind;

this group of kids just had to give the word that it was worth the effort.

For an instant, my eyelids closed and I collected myself. Sensing my seriousness, they all fell quiet and in the foreign hush, I challenged each of my peers to live up to their American honor. My breath caught until I finally dared to look. What I saw was worth the tension: arms began to make their way from laps and tables, moving steadily upwards into the air. Ninety-eight hands answered my question. They were going to do it. I began to pass around the pledge sheets.

There was no need to reinvent the wheel. We could partner with dozens of clubs that already had the capacity to take on new projects. It just meant convincing Student Government, National Honor Society, JRROTC, Hispanic Alliance, Future Business Leaders of America, Debate Team, Fellowship of Christian Athletes, Medical Society, Model United Nations, Students Newspaper, Environment Club, John Adams Historical Society, Young Conservatives, Octagon Club, Passionate Young Democrats, Video Tech, Sisters of Distinction, Dance Team.... whew, we got 'em all.

On September 11, 2002, Sean Maloney - skinny, dark-haired, and perennially decked out in Abercrombie and Fitch - nervously rattled his half-page speech as he waited to talk to the rest of the school over the announcements. For a student body president, used to the spotlight, he recounted, "My heart was racing. Never before had I presented something this big to my student body and at such a delicate moment. Never before had I cared quite so much." His voice might have lost its usual flow as he stumbled over the first few sentences, trying to regain his composure, but he poured every ounce of emotion to prove to one thousand teenagers that this really mattered.

> I kept wondering how much the school had paid attention to my announcement that morning until a tall freshman, without a clue who I was, came up to me with a pledge sheet, saying, 'Hey, how ya' doing? I'm working on this youth movement thing and want you to have this. It's to show our support of democracy after 9/11. All you have to do is have some adults promise their vote by signing it. Sound good?' There was my answer.

Youth-led and youth-driven, Freedom's Answer was our responsibility with our credibility at stake. As we stood before our peers during class or handed them a flyer while in line at lunch, their faces would turn toward us and their eyes would lift to our face. We spoke and they listened. Some were not swayed; some shrugged, a few would raise their eyebrows incredulously and ask, "What's in it for me?" Then the same afternoon, they walked outside and saw the rest of the lunch line out in the streets with clipboards and pens. Then they understood.

We couldn't give up on anyone as a "lost cause," even when it seemed like we just couldn't get through. Michael Brewer of Florida attests to how much a few words to a stranger can mean.

> 'Down with the puppet student government! Viva the Revolution!'

> A classmate of mine shouted these words into the bustling cafeteria of seniors preparing the chicken-wire and streamers for Homecoming. As class president, I would have preferred that he advise me on his views privately instead of yelling into an already stressed-out group of kids, but it seemed

fate was not in my favor. To understand this kid, imagine the typical high school discontent: upset with the world, the country, and, of course, student council.

On September 11, 2002, several weeks earlier, everyone said their Pledge of Allegiance with pride that day, even this guy who was now considering burning his draft card.

I found him outside the cafeteria and talked straight with him. Letting the words just come, I said, 'I get your point, but you have no right to criticize your elected leadership unless you vote or participate to change it. Even you had some pride for your country less than a month ago. There's a Young Voter's Club meeting next Tuesday about a new project that's starting. Be there.' Shocking everyone, he showed up. He became one of our loudest Freedom's Answer activists.

What's more, he received a senatorial nomination to the United States Naval Academy at Annapolis, Maryland, and will attend next year.

This guy wasn't alone. There were hundreds more like him, just needing a shove to get started. How could we pique their interest?

Nationally, we had heard about programs that rocked: a brand new Corvette raffled off as part of what Indiana University called its "Vote Hard" campaign and a Florida State University "Make-Over Night," donated by a national department store for the sorority that registered the most students to vote. On our bare-bones budget, it would be a little hard to pull off something like that. Sharon West, who ice-skates every weekend with a group of Illinois elementary school girls, candidly ruminated, "A patriotic doughnut party was pretty much as far as it went."

During the National Leadership Council conference calls, we asked America's leaders, "What's up with rewards? Do they really work?" The answer was "yes." Rewards, incentives, an immediate benefit for giving up time made kids stop in the hallways and pacify their friends, as they tried to catch the end of the afternoon announcements. The National Leadership Council came up with this:

Top Ten Ways We've Heard
Schools are Selling Freedom's Answer:

10. One week in the #1 reserved spot in the parking lot for the most pledges.
9. Top pledge collector gets to be principal for the day and choose ten friends to switch with faculty.
8. No school uniforms for a month if school reaches 90% participation.
7. Girls challenge boys for most pledges, winners pick band for prom.
6. Winner gets free limo service for two days - to school and back.
5. Each grade level elects a rep that competes for two weeks to get the most pledges. Each morning, in the gym, the principal announces the current stats.
4. Freedom's Answer raffle: winner gets a gourmet lunch.
3. 3-days without homework for the student who signs up other neighborhood schools.
2. Free Sony CD-player for the student who recruits the most other students to participate
1. Top pledge collectors in each grade win a flag from their Member of Congress.

These modest enticements were enough to catch the attention of some who might have otherwise slipped through the cracks. Maybe a few wanted a pizza party so they could get out of first period. Others needed to fulfill their school community service requirements. And although incentives and class obligations drew them in, the dynamism of the project captured them for the long haul. Katie Anderson, a soft-spoken 14-year-old from Colorado who normally prefers to "look rather than lead" describes the lure:

> Freedom's Answer was not an option. My history teacher made the project a requirement using one simple method: the popular cattle prod called 'DO IT OR YOU GET A ZERO.' As if that wasn't enough, he also offered extra credit, which happens about as often as Antarctica reaches 80 degrees. That's really what got me motivated. So honestly, I wasn't attracted to the program itself - originally. I was physically picked up and thrown into it. It was when I got there that I realized, 'What the heck. This is worth the time.'

What started as another grudging obligation - a simple credit fulfillment - became investment and pride in something that could "really happen." We weren't cleaning up rivers that were still being polluted. We weren't holding the hand of an abused kid who was headed back to a broken home. We stopped whitewashing over root causes. Freedom's Answer allowed us to buy into something bigger. It allowed us, with a simple question, to engage every constituent. It showed us the power of mass mobilization and the unlimited potential for change.

People like twelve-year old freshman Doriene Scates, who skipped two grades, started hearing stories from elderly neighbors about the first time they had voted and off-to-college seniors, like seventeen-year-old Kellie Cicconi, watched as their 18-year-old friends filled out their registration forms with pride. "There's something to be said about a project that puts a kid somewhere he doesn't want to be, and then turns him around so much that he keeps coming back for more," she said. Kellie figured that out just like the rest of us.

Most forgot that prizes were even being offered. When interviewed by the local paper, Mr. Nicholas, a history teacher from the south, shrugged happily with a spreading smile, "I told Candice that the minimum was ten pledges - and she came back with 168." The bait became an after-thought and two weeks later when he went back to the kids and gave them their rewards, the response was, "Oh, yeah! It totally slipped my mind. But, uh, thanks."

Sameen Qadir carried a pile of extra pledge sheets throughout the day to try to get more kids onboard. First period, in between classes, during lunch, she could always find someone who was willing to take a sheet and give it a try. One afternoon, she stopped a shy underclassman whom she barely knew:

> Her backpack was as big as she was, but it wasn't the weight of her books alone that seemed to make her shoulders sag. I gently began to tell her about Freedom's Answer, but before I could finish, she pushed the pledge sheet back toward me. 'I'm not in SU [student union] or any of that,' she said.
>
> I shook my head, 'What you're in or not in has noth-ing to do with Freedom's Answer. Anyone can take these papers and really change something here. Maybe you'd like to give it a shot.' I handed her two forms, thanked her, and made my way down the hall to seek out more recruits.

A few days later, when Sameen went to her advisor's office to pick up the pledge sheets that had been handed in that day, she found the twenty pledges that the same girl had collected. Scrawled on the side of the page was,

"Where can I get more sheets?"

Students across the nation were joining us from the halls. Why not try the classrooms? So asking teachers to lend us class-time, we ushered Freedom's Answer into US History and government courses. Some were thrilled, some were stingy - but Rod Tillman blew us away. Mr. Tillman's social studies classes, 130 students in 5 different periods, made Freedom's Answer a course-wide project. His favorite part? "Only days after it was introduced, they came rushing back in with pointed concerns about the candidates and the issues. They wanted to be ready to answer the questions that adults were asking them as they collected pledges. Because we were talking about the elections in the classroom, they were able to help the voters become informed."

We spend hours a night pouring over textbooks, taking notes on the extraordinary men and women who have preceded us. Rarely are we presented with the chance to shape history ourselves. So government remains something for us to read about, not engage in. Teachers scratch their heads, wondering at our indifference, perhaps failing to realize that to us, the process lived and died well before our time.

Freedom's Answer reached out and pulled us into the middle of what we used to only read about. We inadvertently found ourselves part of the political process that had never included us. We may have forgotten what year Abraham Lincoln was born, or how many elections he lost before he won, but we would always remember what it felt to be a little like him, to shape America into the place we thought it should be.

Execute a Plan

Three principal programs gave every student who signed up specific ways to get the job done. Real and concrete, these were what converted pitch-lines and slogans into votes delivered. When we offhandedly asked a skeptical student body, "Want to break a record?" Adopt a Block, Friday Night Football, and Take Ten formed the "how-to."

Adopt a Block. Cassie Chandler, a dark-haired New Yorker, finds herself ringing doorbells every fall, raising funds for new uniforms or a junior class trip. She despises every minute of it. "Neighbors begin to associate a knock on their doors with the emptying of their wallets. It doesn't occur to them that we would ring a doorbell for any other reason." But then we jumped to the streets, "adopting our blocks," asking that our neighbors support a nation's beliefs instead of the local high school band. Cassie tells it like it is:

> I approached one house on my street and caught a glimpse of my neighbor pressing her face against a windowpane. She watched me walk up the sidewalk and hesitated as she opened the door. I asked her for her signature and she gladly signed my sheet. But still she stood waiting, as if expecting another request. When I thanked her and began to go down her front steps, she called out to me. 'Is that all you needed, Cassie?' she asked. With a smile, I answered, 'That's it.' She waved good-bye, reminded me to come back again soon. And shaking her head, she closed the door.

We tended to startle the people we approached. They weren't used to such simple requests and were even taken aback when we made them, but our sincerity overpowered their hesitance. They couldn't refuse - if they did, they'd be embarrassed. Who wants to admit to a fifteen-year-old neighborhood kid taking the time to visit that they're too busy for America?

Maren Schultz was startled at the impact the program had. Half a nation away from Cassie, she was perpetually busy with activities at Lincoln High, but on a rare day off, she scrimped together enough time to gather pledges from her neighbors. The petite senior - she barely surpasses five feet - expected neighbors to rush to the dotted line, but she found the unexpected:

> I had been so busy throughout the fall that there just hadn't been time to go door to door until one afternoon in the middle of October. I zipped up my jacket and grabbed an Adopt a Block sheet, glad to finally be able to dedicate some time. But 15 minutes and 4 houses later, my paper was as empty as before. It's not that my neighbors refused to vote, it was just that someone else had already rung their doorbells and asked them.

Students in her school had been given a goal and a way of reaching it, and they had answered that call. Maren: "I had to laugh. We had specifically told them what to do, and they had gone out and done it. A clear objective was easy for my school to reach."

Of course, Adopt a Block wasn't right for every neighborhood. Some were too dangerous for anyone to go door-to-door. And principal/teacher Robby Sauer's eight-member senior class faced different difficulties:

> The Adopt a Block program was not very realistic for our very rural, sprawling community. One stu-

dent, Jeremy, was determined to find a way for us to participate. So he came up with a new class motto, and in the process made Freedom's Answer workable for our class. He suggested that we 'Adopt a Country Mile' instead. The voting in our county went up this year from 58% in the 1998 mid-term election to 66% on November 5th. I am confident that Freedom's Answer, and our creativity, contributed to that increase.

We spent hours after school and on the weekends adopting everything in sight. The one-on-one interaction was moving, but there was another place we knew well where Americans congregate by the millions each autumn weekend.

Friday Night Football. From September to November, maybe even longer if our team plays well, cheers explode into the brisk night, stadium lights glare from afar, and teens and adults alike begin the weekend with a football game. We swamp our stadiums to cheer on "the boys" and pour into concession stands to warm hands during halftime. What better place to seek out hundreds of earnest citizens than the stands of America's stadiums? Was there anything more American than Friday Night Football? Stephanie Fergason tells how Center Grove High School rallied its community in Greenwood, Indiana:

> I stood before this canvas, this beautiful poster, smeared with paint and names and promises that we had filled in only a matter of hours. One by one, we asked people coming into the football game to add their signatures to the hanging, to reaffirm their belief in American liberties. And one by one they took the pens from our hands and added their names to what was now a masterpiece of our democracy. Heaped in every available space, names of all sizes,

scripts, and colors blurred together, as diverse as the throngs that signed them. Those people promised us their vote and reestablished faith in our government as something worth protecting - and all by writing their names on a canvas.

Scores will be forgotten, rivalries will slacken, and the memories of a winning touchdown will fade as rapidly as the stadium lights shut down after a game. But some experiences last. "I don't remember who won the game that night," Stephanie admits. "But I can tell you story after story about the people I collected pledges from."

We stood ready and waiting as rosy-cheeked crowds flooded in before the first quarter kick-off or clamored for hot dogs during halftime. "Even if the season isn't going well, the crowd is always excited, ready for action," says 16-year-old Vidya Gunasekaran of West High School in upstate New York. "We knew that this was the perfect time to harness that energy and make it serve a higher purpose." Advisor Tami Curley of Sparks High School in Washoe County Nevada agreed:

> One of my students, Lydia, was waiting to give a flier to a lady at the front gate. 'What do I win?' asked the excited parent before taking the flier. Lydia smiled and answered with enthusiasm, 'The right to vote!' The woman responded, 'Great!' took the flier, and went into the game.

We channeled that Friday night energy and directed it towards a greater purpose. "As a junior in high school, I never would have thought that I could make history with a few words and handshakes," said Courtney Summerskill, a student at Mill Valley High School in Shawnee, Kansas. "That was all it took." Our high school stadiums became the home for our high school crusades.

Take Ten. Adopt a Block sent us into our neighborhoods. Friday Night Football hurled us into the middle of crowds. Take Ten was our chance to bring along the people we already knew best. Between mom and dad, grandparents, and friends 18 and older, every high schooler knows at least ten adults well enough to ask them to vote. Even better, we hoped these adults would be ashamed if they didn't follow through with their promise.

Many high school efforts with Take Ten trickled down to our younger brother and sisters. Middle school teacher Sabrina McCartney distributed Take Ten sheets to her Odessa, Florida, classes and was astounded.

> Matt is a seventh grader in my first period geography class and could not wait to get started having people sign up on his Take-Ten sheet. Even though I warned my students that it would be difficult to get other teachers and people on campus to sign the papers because they could only sign one student's sheet, Matt decided to ask numerous individuals around campus immediately. He convinced other teachers, support staff and parent volunteers to sign on. Before the day was over, Matt had completed his sheet and asked for another one to take home.

Kathy Ojeda of Connecticut sat in her social studies class at the beginning of October, barely appearing to listen as her teacher explained his latest extra credit assignment - pledge collecting. But a few days later, Kathy's foster mom came into the class for a parent-teacher conference. "She thanked me repeatedly for introducing the project," wrote teacher Edward Hogan, "because thanks to Kathy's efforts, she and her husband were now registered voters for the first time."

The freshman who collected six pledges because he was excited about an election or the sixteen-year-old who convinced her mother to cast a vote for the first time - they were adding to a tally that *could* produce a record vote.

We had taken a national goal and broken it into tangible steps, which helped us meet our local aspirations. And yet Freedom's Answer remained flexible. Boys Nation President Brad Johnson constantly kept the National Advisory Council focused on a "keep it simple" philosophy that emphasized the grassroots. There were no quotas and no requirements that any school follow our programs. Every school could build a project customized to its specific community. Voter turnout would flourish when each school team coordinated an outreach effort that spoke to its own collective personality.

Versatility meant teachers brought it into their classrooms. It meant geeks, jocks, and leaders alike grabbed pledge forms from our stacks. After learning about Freedom's Answer, student council president Kellie Cicconi's high school decided to undertake the project in its first attempt with a national movement. Initially hesitant, she was unsure a "big" national program would work in such a small school:

> To my surprise, on my first day, I collected 50 pledges, which is a lot considering we only have about 60 people of voting age in my school. I couldn't believe how adamant some people were about exercising their right to vote. My student council then decided to push the program at our Open House. We got over 100 signatures. I don't think I have felt more proud of anything that our student council has done before that night. At first,

> I didn't think that we, being such a small school, could ever make any really big national program work. But Freedom's Answer taught me that even small communities can get involved. And sometimes, because we're small and are ignored so much, it's even more important that we do.

Much larger Shawnee Mission West High School reinforced its own Take Ten efforts by bringing candidates into the classroom. They found that giving the school an up-close glimpse of people who were running in the election increased the relevance of Freedom's Answer.

Three basic ideas spun-off into different variations and eager representatives sent emails out to kids across the nation, saying, "Ohh... try this" or "Man, this idea rocks." Our loose framework was sweeping America, providing substantial suggestions to all schools, but also allowing new ideas to spill forth. Some districts didn't have football games; others lacked the funds to photocopy pledge sheets. We had to work with what we had. We were forced to turn barriers that blocked us into bridges that led to new techniques.

Every kid, regardless of the crowd he traveled in or the GPA on her transcript, could pick up a pledge sheet and collect a few signatures. What other project invited both the student body president and the student in after-school detention to rally behind a common cause? Extending our outreach had broadened our base. Giving kids pledge sheets locked it in.

Involve the Community

While we strove to ring every doorbell and cover every block, we also needed a visible community presence to gain momentum. If everyone was talking "'bout those kids axing for ma vote," even our neighbor who was never home couldn't escape us. So students streamed to events that would draw crowds and pick-up pledges. We would miss people - parents rushing through the lobby after a band concert or morning shoppers hurrying out of the mall with a packed schedule. Certainly, we couldn't stop them all, but we could be the last thing that they saw on their way out the door.

Dominique Scott of West Chicago went to her school's Parent Night to collect pledges. "A ton of parents came up to congratulate us after we had set up our booth. Even if we hadn't talked to them, they remembered seeing the table and remembered to vote because of it. They were so glad that someone was finally doing something like this," she remembered.

Vidya Gunasekaran worked for three hours at her school's open house, stopping parents at the door as they came into the lobby to pick up flyers and class schedules. She wrote:

> 'Have you already signed a voting pledge?' 'That's right, on Election Day, November 5.' 'Name here, sign here, please.' 'We'll send you a reminder just to make sure.' Such requests reverberated throughout my high school's lobby as parents streamed into the building for our early October Open House. We, the Freedom's Answer Youth Corps of West High, had lapsed into a reassuring pattern as we made our way around to all who passed through the door.

Vidya and friends were really rolling… fifty pledges, then seventy-five; within the first thirty minutes, they easily surpassed 100. A young single mother scribbled her name in seconds and then a frazzled father, still wearing his suit from work, signed. A "deeply touched" and "just dog-gone inspired" elderly grandmother laid her sheet on the growing pile of completed forms and sweetly rambled about "young people with such dear hearts." Shortly after, Vidya was startled to see a man hurriedly burst through the door and blow past her. Despite the 6 o'clock crowd, she got in a quick "excuse me, sir," and caught up with him, a Take Ten sheet in hand. Vidya recounts:

> He interrupted me mid-sentence. 'Who do I have to vote for?'
>
> I was taken aback by his gruffness. 'Well that part's completely your decision.'
>
> The man's eyes narrowed and his tone became skeptical. 'I don't understand. What's in this for you?'
>
> I hesitated, and seeing this, the man began to turn away. 'I'm only sixteen,' I started. He paused for a moment to turn and look back at me. 'I can't vote, but I believe it's one of the greatest rights that we have. People everywhere have died for such a right. And while I can't yet vote, you can, so the next best thing that I can do is to ask you to vote instead.'
>
> The man shook his head and continued on his way, calling over his shoulder, 'I'm sorry, but no. Try someone else.' There was nothing I could do. I could feel my cheeks redden as I sighed and looked dismally down at my blank sheet.

As the event ended, Vidya was stacking papers and gathering her things when she looked up to find the same man standing next to her:

> Hands in pockets, shuffling his feet, he kept his

eyes on the ground. 'I was just wondering - you still collecting those pledges?'

Taken aback, I nodded and handed him a page. 'Name here, sign here, please.' I must have said those same words a hundred times before, but even to my own ears, they now seemed entirely new. As the man walked away, he once again called something over his shoulder, 'This is a nice thing you kids are doing here. Good luck with it.'

Freedom's Answer was transforming young and old alike. AnnMarie Colucci went directly to the adults, leaving her school to visit a local veteran's center. After she spoke about Freedom's Answer, one World War II Vet asked if he could say a few words before the meeting was closed. Recalled AnnMarie:

He stood up, leaned on his cane and walked slowly to the front of the room. He looked upon his friends, and spoke: 'Before today, I feared for the future of America. I did not believe that today's teens would stand up for what I fought to protect. That all changed as I sat listening to this representative for Freedom's Answer. I discovered that teens share the same will to defend freedom that I do. The single greatest strength of the United States of America does not lie in its military, but rather in the will of its people to protect freedom at any cost. When high school-aged teens, who cannot, for the most part, even vote, will throw themselves so wholeheartedly into a movement such as Freedom's Answer, I no longer fear for the future, but am overjoyed that tomorrow will, by all indications, be even brighter than today.'

One student, taking only an hour of her day, was able to clear an entire room of misconceptions about our generation. We approached adults who had refused to vote for twenty years and walked away with their signatures in hand.

Haydde Gonzalez attends Francis Poly High School in Sun Valley, California. Described by her advisor as a "one-woman crusade," she became an articulate spokesperson for voting and for freedom as she worked to register voters in her Hispanic community. She appeared at the school's Parent Night to secure pledges from every eligible adult she could find. Then she downloaded the appropriate registration forms in English *and* in Spanish to help nearly a dozen new voters register. And all of this was punctuated by one astonishing fact: Haydde is not even an American citizen. She resides in the United States on a student visa.

We may have used what we had, but we also had to work around what we didn't have. More than anything, that meant time. The weeks unraveled quickly while we rushed from club meetings to practices to the piles of homework accumulating in our backpacks. We had two options: hide behind our schedules or accept the challenge.

With only one game left in the season, Katherine Roland of Ponca City, Oklahoma, mobilized a handful of students into action. Understaffed and overloaded, she used the time and resources available, surprising herself with what she could do:

> We printed out way more flyers than we thought we'd ever need (wishful thinking, I guess), and little pledge cards, that simply stated, 'I, _____, as a dedicated American citizen, pledge to participate in the election on Tuesday, November 5.' The night arrived, and wouldn't ya believe it, we got rid of (and received back!) all except about 20 of those lit-

tle cards we gave out. We were so excited. Despite all of the obstacles we had to overcome (having a small membership, all of the members being so busy, organizing our Friday Night Football so 'late in the game' - no pun intended) we accomplished our goals and ended up with way more votes than we could ever have imagined. Plus, the voter turnout in our city increased. It just goes to show that a good cause, a little elbow grease, and a lot of heart can make a huge impact, even if you only have a few to do the job.

Make a Personal Connection.

Impersonal technology dominates our lives. You call customer service lines to hear an automated voice at the other end with seventeen easy options. You drive to bank ATMs rather than talk to a teller. It's efficient, but remote. And voting had become much the same way - until we determined to change it.

"High tech, high touch" was our mantra. We logged on to freedomsanswer.net to stay updated, but we knocked on doors and made personal phone calls to ask the adults to vote. Before Election Day, citizens are flooded with electronic phone calls and distant handouts. In order to combat an apathetic American public, we had to capitalize on the mistakes that were being made in a technology and advertising-driven world. That meant pounding some pavement, shaking a few hands, and knocking on doors like an old-fashioned campaign. It had been easy for indifferent voters to ignore a process that treated them as numbers instead of individuals.

Michael Brewer, a senior in Fort Lauderdale, Florida, used a personal story to command the attention of those he asked to pledge.

> My father just became a U.S. citizen a few years
> ago. He has always, always had an enormous
> respect for America and its freedoms, which has
> only increased now that he can partake in those
> rights. This was my way to honor my dad - to
> honor his beliefs, his sacrifices. To honor who he
> is.

Mike's father had taught him to value democracy and when he recounted his story, it won people over. "When they heard what I asked, they swore they'd be at the polls."

Stories became the sustenance along the road to making history. Smashing the record was a goal, but how it happened was most important. Exclamations of, "I signed up a woman who hasn't voted in twelve years!" or "I talked to my grandfather for two hours about World War II after he signed a pledge," became common. We still wanted enough pledges to do our part in tackling the record. But we were no longer just burying a statistic. We were sending apathy to an early grave.

In her neighborhood, Kim Dowgiallo of Pennsylvania went door-to-door to add signatures to her pledge sheets, and was disappointed to learn that her neighbors didn't vote. "They didn't think anyone cared." Yet the same people who adamantly refused to go to the polls were willing to listen to a teenager who earnestly asked them to reconsider.

> I stood at the doorstep while an elderly lady faced
> me from inside. She was somewhere in her late six-
> ties, gray-haired, hard-faced, and with her arms
> crossed. I doubted that she would listen for very
> long. I had nothing to lose, so I began to speak just

to see how long I could keep her from shutting the door. I told her about Freedom's Answer and she uncrossed her arms. I told her about why I cared so much about her vote and her face softened. The more I spoke, the more she listened.

A few minutes later, she admitted that she had been planning to give me every excuse in the book to avoid voting, and even would have agreed just so that I would go away. But after meeting me face-to-face on her doorstep, she looked me square in the eye. 'Well Kim,' she said, 'maybe it is time to register. If someone your age can care so much, then I guess it's the duty of someone my age to care even more.'

In the weeks before Election Day, America's voters receive automated phone calls reminding them to vote; generic flyers are plastered to their car windows and sheets jammed into their mailboxes. But how many times can they remember being personally asked to go to the polls? As Dominique Scott said, "Adults were surprised to hear me giving them a call, startled even that someone would care enough to individually ask them to vote."

Getting Close

One million students, fifty states, and thousands and thousands of towns spanned the nation. And one program, one movement could be adopted into every single one. We would explain the versatility to newspapermen covering this "nice little project" of ours for the weekly community section and outline the idea to TV reporters as they asked for an explanation. Smiling gently with a look of haughty self-importance smeared across their faces, they would pat our heads and encourage us to "keep dreaming big." Now it was our turn to roll our eyes. They had no idea.

The media wasn't there on the first anniversary of September 11th, when on a field outside of Raleigh's Broughton High the silence of 2000 students threaded the student body.

They weren't there in rural Odessa, New York, where its forty students made freedom and its answer ring in all five school hallways.

They weren't at South Shore High in Brooklyn where the football team and its fans remembered their fallen friend and coach and fireman.

They weren't in Anna Friedinger's gym in Pekin when 2200 students kicked off Freedom's Answer in their first school-wide assembly in five years.

They weren't there in Cleveland, Tennessee to watch a young boy turn around his life.

How could *they* know that the dream was national and that records would fall?

Just Three

Chapter 5

Danny

South Shore High School's Assistant Football Coach, Danny Suhr, a member of the New York City Fire Department, was one of the first to arrive at the World Trade Towers on 9-11. He was also one of the first fire-fighters to die. Before he could even put on his equipment, he was hit by a body falling from the building and instant-ly killed. In emotional interviews, Coach Charles Gomes and seventeen-year-old Anthony Owens recount how the one-hundred players of the football program at South Shore High, dedicated Freedom's Answer to the legacy of "Coach Danny".

Coach Charles Gomes:

> Danny had been a NYC firefighter for at least fifteen years and volunteered with the local football team here at South Shore because he couldn't think of a better way to spend his days off of work. He was a 6'2" guy... really solid, with a hulking back and a great smile, pretty much an all-American hero. His friends called him Captain America because he would do any-thing to help anybody. When he passed away, it was devastating for the kids, coaches, and the school community. He had been a face they could depend on, a guy who they went to when there wasn't anybody else who would listen. After his death, we were looking for a way to

honor Danny and we found Friday Night
Football with Freedom's Answer... it was our
chance to say goodbye, our chance to say thank
you. For every varsity game, home or away,
the JV players and cheerleaders would stand
outside the gate as people came in and convince them to pledge to vote. Each of them carried a picture of Danny, on the back of their
clipboards or pinned to their shirts as reminder
of his memory.

Senior Anthony Owens:

I grew up in a pretty rough Brooklyn neighborhood but not as rough as some. South Shore is
a big school, but it's a regular high school, just
like yours, just like anyone's. The teachers are
just like everyone's teachers; they try to make
you do what you gotta do. And kids, kids are
the same everywhere.

The football here is real good ... real good.
That's what everyone says. Every Saturday, the
team goes to a park to play football, we train
year-round, whether it's football season or not.
We're all pretty close; it's a family here. We
respect each other. You just don't let other people mess with your family...

When I first met Coach Danny, he came with us
to football camp. We were so tired, because
we'd been practicing for days and days without
a break. And so Coach Danny is like, I'm going
to talk to [head coach] Salvado, get you the
night off. And he did. Man, he came through
for us. He really did. I will always remember
that.

When he got killed in 9-11, that just hurt our
family. I'd never seen Salvado cry, only a little
at senior banquets and stuff. But he cried and

cried that day. Coach Danny was there when we needed him. He was a firefighter and had a lot of stuff to deal with, but he took the time to work with us, and that meant something.

After he died, I watched TV and I saw stories about him. They said that he was this All-American football player, this really good guy. There was a lot I didn't know about his life, but they got that part right. He was a good guy. That's when everything hit me, when I saw it all on TV. I was like man, that's Coach Danny, that's our coach.

Freedom's Answer kinda came out of nowhere. A guy came around during the summer and told us about the program and how they needed some kids to go around to ask people to vote. It was my first time doing anything like that; I'd never done community service before. It was just a couple of hours and six kids that first time. Now we've got the entire school helping.

I will definitely be a voter now. Since Freedom's Answer, I'm loving history. I never thought about it before, until now; it was never an option until now. I'm even loving politics. I watch President Bush on the news every night giving his speeches and then I turn off the TV and I think about it. That never would have happened before. It's not the kind of thing that you usually hear about at South Shore. But… but I think Coach would have been proud.

Anna

This story and the poem that follows it are from Anna Freidinger, a Girls Nation Senator from Illinois, and a senior at Pekin Community High School. Earlier in the year, she was asked to offer a personalized quote for the Freedom's Answer website. Her response was: "I believe mobilizing the vote starts with mobilizing people's hearts." Little did she know her own heart would be touched so deeply.

I was at the Senior Citizens Center asking the residents if they would pledge to vote in the upcoming election, when an elder gentleman said he would like to. He could barely walk down the hall... let alone the stairs to the polling place. I thanked him and explained our goal to him and why we felt the cause was so important.

After I finished my explanation, the man smiled and said that even though it was incredibly difficult for him, he would get to the polls on the 5th. I told him I understood if he was unable to pledge, but he said he thought it was amazing that it meant so much to someone who was not yet old enough to vote, and since he could, he would cast his vote in my honor.

Hearing him pledge in spite of his difficulties made me realize there are many people fighting for our freedom just by simply going to a polling place. The elderly gentleman touched my life in a way I had not been expecting, and even if his single voice was not heard around the world on Election Day, it was heard in me and for that, I thank him.

A Declaration of Independence (and gratitude)

True
pride   comes
from   -^-exercising-^-
-the freedom-   we are given
and   defending
it   with .
all that   -we-
have.   True courage
comes   from listening to
economists   then hearing the
national anthem and having faith;
even when you are unsure of what
is to come. And the true reward is found
within the sparkling eyes   and beaming
smiles of American   youth who
still have the freedom to   express
their gratitude. It is for this
America has cast their vote.
The American dream can
not be secure in our sleep
without the countless people
who awaken early in the
morning just to rekindle
the spirit of our liberty by
going   to   the   polls.
Thank you for igniting
The flame of freedom.
And allowing the torch
To be passed along to the next generation.
It is for this our country will never forget
the sentences you have allowed to be written
in the ongoing Declaration of our Independence.

Thank you
For voting.

-Anna Freidinger

Johnny

Johnny Ramsey, a stocky black seventh grader at Cleveland Middle School in Cleveland, Tennessee, was suspended during the beginning of 2002 for fighting. The fourteen year old had a history of getting into trouble at school, lived in an inner city slum, and in the words of one educator, "had been pretty much written off by most teachers." Four months later, he told us Freedom's Answer had turned his life around:

One teacher, Ms. Janis Kyser, talked to all of us in a school assembly about voting and ways that we could be involved as young people. I went home and told my parents and grandparents about Freedom's Answer and they pretty much laughed at me. They all told me that there was no need to vote because their voice didn't count anyway. I asked them why and they said that at one time they were not allowed to vote where they lived, so they had never bothered to register. My Granddaddy said that he had really forgot that he could vote.

I talked to my Grandmother about it and she said that if Granddaddy didn't vote, then she shouldn't either. Then of course, my parents had never registered to vote, because their parents had not voted.

I came back to school and asked Ms. Kyser what I had to do to help my grandparents and parents become registered voters. She gave me some papers to take home for them to fill out. I helped my grandparents and my parents fill out the papers, brought them back to Ms. Kyser and she turned them in.

I was real excited because I helped my parents get so they could vote. This felt really good to me. I decided that if I could help my folks vote, then I could help others also. Ms. Kyser and I talked about it for a long time and I took her challenge to get 10 people to pledge to vote. I wrote a practice speech and rehearsed it with her. Without voting, other people accept leadership someone else chose. If you choose not to vote, you give up your right to choice.

The speech was real easy. I told them about my grandparents and parents and asked them to vote for me since I was not old enough to vote, to use their voice and be heard. I decided that I could get most of the people who lived in my neighborhood. Ms. Kyser told me not to be disappointed if some of them did not pledge to vote. We talked about what I would say if people questioned me about Freedom's Answer and why it was important in my life and how important it was in their lives.

I found that many black people did not know the importance of voting. Well, now at least 187 people in my neighborhood know the importance of voting. I had 187 people pledge to vote. I helped lots of people register to vote, helped to arrange transportation for people who could not go vote by themselves and talked to other people at my school about volunteering in their neighborhood.

Johnny raced home from school after cross-country practice each day to go door - to - door, despite intimidation from gang members who thought he was working with the police. He talked with other students, helping convince 800 of 1100 sixth, seventh, and eighth graders at Cleveland Middle School to participate in Freedom's Answer. Many of them registered voters at Wal-Mart booths, the mall, football games, and did neighborhood canvassing in addition to Take Ten. On Election Day, Johnny spent his entire day watching over 75 of his neighbors' houses, while they went to the polls, to ensure they weren't robbed - a favor many of his pledgers requested.

The condition of our neighborhood makes it even more important that we vote. We have gangs all around and three people were just shot from drug deals. But I learned that teachers recognize me when I use my voice in a different way. Freedom's Answer showed me that I can be a part of something, other than being involved in a gang.

The expectation in my neighborhood is to be bad. The boys know I run track, they talk smack and try to fight me. But I have more going for my life now than fighting.

My entire life has changed... even before I got to middle school, I got in trouble for not doing work. Now, I have accepted responsibility, even though my boys call me uppity and put me down. But I've got better things to worry about now.

Johnny was recently chosen to serve on a top school panel as a representative of all 7th graders in the school. Janis Kyser's last thought: "Johnny Ramsey is going to make it. There is not a doubt in my mind."

The Final Countdown

Chapter 6

The week before the election was brimming with constant anticipation. We had been drawn in by Freedom's Answer; it had captured our imagination; we were emotionally connected. We had sacrificed heart and soul for our mission, but in the back of every head, hidden behind the hours already invested, was a nagging question: "We had worked so hard, but was it all worth it?" No one knew for sure, but with each new school and each pledge signed, we were building a fortress in modern political society incomprehensible to armchair critics.

In almost three thousand schools, there were hundreds of thousands of stories. We had connected with a non-voter, convinced a friend to register, or planned a rally. But no matter our experience, when the leaves fell in early November, we stood united. Peppered throughout the country, most of us were strangers, yet despite different ideas, ages, and schools, we had banded together.

A rush of adrenaline, excitement, and apprehension descended on many students as the final week crept up behind them. The last days would prove to be the battleground for the September 11 Generation, the warriors defending democracy. We rallied the troops, smeared the war paint (this time in red, white and blue), and marched into battle.

Crunchtime Projects

We are scripted the "Procrastination Generation." Instead of spending two weeks hunched over a stack of books in a library with bloodshot eyes and a throbbing head, we have 0.4-second Google searches producing millions of possibilities. As our parents go off to bed, muttering that we should do the same, we press on, still earning bloodshot eyes and the throbbing headache despite the utility of modern technology. We have the option to delay, until we hit crunch time, usually 11:47 on a Sunday night or a jerky Monday morning bus ride.

Likewise, in the week before Tuesday, November 5, the looming deadline was unavoidable. The trick was to sustain the energy of those already working, while bringing in the late arrivals who were jolted to attention by the upcoming election. Sure, we had football games, pep rallies, and vocabulary tests to worry about, but something about "6 days away" awakened many of our slow-moving peers.

Bryce Mendez, a Hawaiian junior, forfeited many fall activities to focus on involving Hawaii schools - all of them. The boyish Pacific Islander isn't a particularly commanding presence, until you find out that the groundwork he laid throughout autumn involved 93% of all Hawaiian schools. With seven days and counting, Bryce stood ready to overwhelm voters in the week before the polls opened. Just as any leader should do, he relied on a network of his classmates interested in the project - instilling in them ownership that multiplied into a vibrant statewide team. Though many said he couldn't overcome the "indifference" of his laid back state's attitude towards politics, Bryce's group had the infrastructure in place to mount an impressive last-minute drive.

They started by calling every number in the phone book. Bryce explains, "We repeated the same phrase: "Aloha, on behalf of Freedom's Answer and the Hawaii State Student Council, we would like to remind you to go and vote November 5th, Mahalo for your time." One name multiplied into thousands as Hawaiian students ditched the beaches to paste phones against their ears throughout the week. Just days after rounds of time-consuming calls, the determination of Bryce and his colleagues was tested while standing on a downtown street corner. With confused faces staring back at them, they waved handmade posters at passing cars.

> We went to a local grocery store to wave signs on the busy street during traffic hour. At a time when most people are focused on getting home, we knew the task would be onerous. We continued throughout the November afternoon, waving and yelling as if we were cheering at a football game though we were simply reminding people to vote. As we were leaving, one woman, who had passed earlier, pulled up and thanked us for the reminder. She told us, 'If you hadn't reminded me, I wouldn't have voted.'

Greg Teich, a popular senior from Massachusetts, seems like the polar opposite of dark, skinny Bryce. More laid-back than his constantly driven west-coast colleague, he casually ambles through his high school halls, slapping fives with the other cool kids. Would the Captain of the Wrestling Team risk tarnishing his reputation or missing a Friday night hook-up to plug a program such as this? "I felt a calling," he said. "Occasionally a program so vast and so right, absolutely captivates us and even if it means stepping out from your peers, you have to lead." Greg illustrated his first step against the norm on a drizzly day in late October:

> I pulled a chair into the middle of one of the lobbies at my school during a passing time between two periods, and climbed atop it. With questioning stares, the rest of the school eyed me. At this point, I started my speech, booming in a rich, echoing voice so that anyone not listening had to. 'Do you love your country? Do you remember when the towers fell?'
>
> It was as if someone had slapped me and I was responding to the sting; that sting was 9-11. The teachers stood at their doors, some laughing, others shaking their heads, but the students were still and silent. I wasn't quite sure what their response would be, but I explained Freedom's Answer anyway. Finally, I dropped the pile of 200 flyers onto the floor, I got down and walked away, never once turning around or lifting my head. Everyone was still for a second. Then the teachers started to clap. One person moved for the flyers and then another, and then came the rush. All that was left in the lobby was the chair I had been orating from.

Just days after his plea for assistance atop the wobbly steel chair, Greg recalls another instance:

> About twenty minutes after I got home from an afternoon soccer game. I had comfortably landed on my kitchen floor, my shin guards and shoes still intact. I previously promised my friend that I would be at her birthday party, but with hundreds of Freedom's Answer envelopes to stuff, I had to tell her that I couldn't make it. She said she understood, with a hint of disappointment in her murmur, and I promised to make it up to her.

> Then I began to get to work. It was 6:15 when I
> started the work and only 7:15 when we finished. A
> band of energetic teenagers arrived at my doorstep
> at 6:30. They said that when my friend told every-
> one else what I was doing, they all just thought for
> a moment and realized that they wanted to help. So
> they came. Each hand grabbed for more envelopes
> and together we finished the job.

Greg's friends understood the importance of the project, so they adopted it as their own. Vicki, Greg's close
friend, said, "We knew it was something special, but we
didn't know how to help. I guess all he needed was an
extra hand." Greg was thankful for the relief and realized
that leading is more than inspiring - it is also involving.

Tom Brown, a Pennsylvanian, paralleled Greg's know-
how, but he didn't wait for friends to flock to his side.
Instead, Tom took the initiative to gather an army of fol-
lowers. The clean-cut Future Business Leader of America
member knew that for a chance at real accomplishment, he
had to have backing from his peers. So he asked for their
help - the ones he threw his first baseball with, the ones he
sat next to in English, and the ones who will walk next to
him on graduation day. It didn't matter who they were or
what they could do, but rather that they do something.
Tom explains one attempt to reach students:

> Shining lights, thumping bass, and chatting students
> surrounded me at our high school's annual
> Activities Fair. Every year, students flock to the Fair
> during their lunch periods to sign up for the coming
> year's exploits. I came to the National Honor
> Society's table, not expecting much interest in
> Freedom's Answer, due to the flashy advertisements
> for sports and doughnuts at the DECA table. I

looked down to search for the obviously hidden pile of "Take Ten" pledge sheets that had been casually left in a corner but to my shock and satisfaction, they were all gone. I looked across the table and names scrawled in black ink, gel ink, and pencil streamed down the front and back of the sign-up sheet. There were so many signatures that torn notebook sheets had to be stapled to the unfolding scroll. A smile crept across my face. In spite of doubts from many Americans as to our generation's civic responsibility, in spite of many distractions my school proved it was willing to support something bigger than ourselves, America.

In North Carolina, Leigh Fowlkes, a bubbly cheerleader, promoted activities throughout her high school. She planned a "car painting event" and plastered "Vote November 5th" on bumpers, doors, and windows. Instead of school colors and streamers highlighting their cars before the late October rival game, students showed their spirit in different colors - America's colors.

Mississippian Jynette Guerra labored to bridge a gap in her local schools. Jynette succeeded in including the often-underestimated Educable Mentally Retarded students. With an accent she admits, "I thought I had included just about everyone in my area, but I had overlooked an important group." Jynette explains, "These kids took pride in their ability to help because it is one thing they could do on their own." She remembers their contribution in the week before Election Day:

I walked into the room, not sure if they could help, but once I saw the look in their eyes and the sincerity of their touch, I knew it was worth it. There were only a few days left before the election and I wanted to get more people roped in so I introduced

Freedom's Answer to the students in the special
education class at our local junior high school.
Each student, not sure how to respond, because they
had never been asked, took a 'Take Ten' flyer to get
their family and friends to sign up. The next day I
came back to the school, hoping for one, maybe two
forms filled out. I walked into the class and to my
surprise, there lay a stack of pledge forms. Each
student had brought one back, and today, they
looked me in the eyes, said 'thank you,' and asked
for another.

Disabled kids are often written off with hushed snickers by other high schoolers, but Jynette clasped their hands and pulled them into the process. The students brought in over 30 pledge sheets - reminding more than 300 people to vote.

In the small Nevada valley of Pahrump, Aynsley Sutherland, the youngest of four girls, gathered her friends and decided to make over 15,000 reminder calls to voters. In the last week, they started from the top of the list, only getting through half of the A's in the first day. The next day more friends appeared, and with phones glued to their ears, the calls multiplied. They didn't reach each voter - a goal they thought was "absolutely impossible" - but they contacted nearly 14,000. They didn't do the "absolutely impossible," merely the "unthinkable."

We tirelessly asked our friends and family to vote, but we still heard the murmurs of disbelief and saw the bewilderment. Even some of our best friends rolled their eyes when we talked about voting. Just like anything, some always care and some always don't. We never expected to reach them all, but it was the ones we found in the middle ground - the kids on the fence - who made our work meaningful.

David Parker, a home-schooled jeans-and-T-shirt kinda guy, drew in a skeptical friend to Freedom's Answer. With a slight country twang, he relates:

> His reply to everything I said concerning the subject, remained the same: 'I don't like the way things are run, so why should I get involved?' I was determined to find a way to prove that he had the power to change what he didn't like - and that voting was part of that process. A few days before elections, I was at a town historical committee meeting where a vote was being taken on the demolition of an old house. We used to play in that house. I still remember the third board to the left by the window in the hallway has a creak that would always scare the girls. Every year on Halloween, we would dress up the abandoned place and make a haunted house where we could scare all our friends. We all really loved the house, especially my skeptical friend. The committee resolved to demolish the house - but by only one vote - a vote any citizen, adult or student alike, could have cast. I visited him the next day, and explained what had happened. On November 5th, my friend was first in line to vote.

Throughout history, issues of extraordinary importance have been decided by a single ballot. One vote elected Hitler as Chancellor of Germany; one vote acquitted President Andrew Johnson after his impeachment; five hundred votes decided the 2000 presidential election. David witnessed just one of them and he became convinced of his importance as a citizen. While his friend seemed to have taken away the same lesson, we often talked to people who just flat out refused to stand up and be counted.

Rejection can slam your toes and chip your ego and each student had his or her own story. Lindsay Ullman, a tiny upstate New York optimist, encountered a couple, marred by the political system, that to this day still refuse to vote. Lindsay explains her encounter:

I clung to the clipboard on this bitter night as doggedly as I had clung to this cause these past few weeks. I really wanted to go home and crawl into bed, but instead I found myself on a corner at the center of town, amongst the 6 o'clock rush hour. Looking down at my sheets, I saw that my hands had turned an angry, biting red as they struggled against the stubborn New York fall. 'Just a few more pledges,' I thought, as I watched the bustle slow to a comfortable trickle this night before Election Day. 'Just a few more.'

A smiling couple strode by as I stood stomping my feet against the chill, and I routinely asked that they add their signatures to my paper. The woman slowly started to shake her head. 'This is all very nice,' she explained, 'but who I vote for makes absolutely no difference. I appreciate that you care, but you won't change my mind.'

People were streaming around us as we stood in the middle of the sidewalk, hurrying expectantly toward their own warm homes. Exhausted, I thanked the couple anyway and turned away, but was stopped before I went very far. 'I may not be able to sign your pledge,' the woman conceded, 'but if there was anything in the past ten years that has made me even want to think about voting, this is it.' I looked at her and nodded, then watched the pair disappear into the fading light of November 4. While the conversation may not have ended as I wanted it to, this was at least a beginning. And, strangely enough, the icy night didn't seem quite so unbearable anymore.

We weren't worried about "no's." We knew that they would come. Our wounds would heal, but Election Day wouldn't wait, so we kept on testing our will. We gave all of ourselves to the project, though we realized that disappointment would inevitably thwart our path. Logically we knew that voting and participation bettered democracy, but what carried us through frustration, tight schedules, and cold nights was our emotional commitment to achieving a national goal by asking for one pledge... and then another. You couldn't help but keep trying, because disappointments aside - there was a glimmer in the eyes of youth once shoved to the curb.

How it Felt

At first Freedom's Answer was a favor a friend had asked us to do, we didn't really get it, and weren't really even sure what "signing up" meant. And then it changed. Once we started calling our friends, and asking for that same favor - we understood.

Colleen Dunn knew what was necessary to make Freedom's Answer work. "We have grown up hearing the stories of our grandparents," Colleen said. "I felt the rough soil of Germany as they explained it and even sometimes heard their cries as they begrudgingly told of their time in the service. I can feel the emotion and try to understand the pain, but to gain their respect was a new challenge." Colleen explains her desire to honor their legacy:

> The cold September rain washes away our tears, as a life of courage, stamina, and dignity is lowered into the earth - a POW of Stalag 17B, my grandfather. With every raindrop, the Honor Guards do not

allow their chins to falter; they remain looking straight ahead and salute a man who gave us freedom. Shivering with emotion, I hold my ten-year-old nephew. Together, we watch as my grandfather is honored for his service to our country. Blood pulses through my veins as the flag is draped over the coffin, lifted, and folded by the soldiers. Overwhelmed with admiration and respect, I stare at the pleats of the red, white, and blue while the words of Grandpa Dan fill my thoughts, 'I wish the youth of today would appreciate and give thanks to the freedoms and liberties soldiers like myself fought for in years past.'

Then, with deep gratitude, I kneel next to the coffin, close to him one last time, and speak aloud, 'Thank you Grandfather.' I stand, look around the National Veterans Cemetery at Cape Cod and see through teary eyes the lines of great men and women's graves, all of whom have sacrificed for America. I say a silent thanks to them as well. At this moment, I am left with a single question: 'What will I do with the gift of life I am still blessed to have?'

Back home at Plymouth, I fulfilled my grandpa's last wishes by galvanizing support, collecting pledges, taking people to the polls on Election Day, showing that I, the posterity of this great nation, do care about its future.

Colleen collected one hundred pledges in the last week before the election, and through each vote on Election Day, she relit the spirit her grandfather had once so gallantly fought for. She confirmed that no matter the perceived chasm between the generations, we still care about our rights, we still care about unity, and we still care about our America.

AnnMarie Colucci, a New Yorker, further explained

such resolve:

> The night was closing as I walked down the poorly lit corridor. I stopped to readjust the overflowing box of pledge forms that slid through my arms and swiped the hair away from my tired face. Just as my hand flicked back my hair, I noticed the names on the list before me. It was there, amid the silence of my empty high school, that it hit me: the simple tasks of copying, distributing, phone calls and emails were negligible compared to what our ancestors endured. I picked up my box and walked down the stairs, now with a clearer vision of my role in our democracy, completely prepared for the final days ahead.

We owed it to America - we all knew that. We owed it to each other - as we were quickly learning. Now we just had to trust ourselves to finish. We had confidence in our peers and we were reaching out to new friends, extending the team in the final days, uncovering new and eager participants all the while. Jonathan Friedman, already the epicenter of Freedom's Answer in Memphis, never once paused in his outreach effort.

> I had been announcing it, pushing it, and getting the word out for weeks. There were flyers on the walls, and announcements every morning and every afternoon. Freedom's Answer was in full swing, but its success was not yet certain. At our student council meeting, I tapped the gavel getting their attention, and the crowd slowly went silent. I thanked them for their attendance, then, without hesitation, rose and gave a last passionate address. 'Friends, we are the September 11 Generation,' I said, 'now is our chance to show the world that we are leaders, we are patriots, and we care about our nation.' I went on for a few more minutes and then, as flyers cir-

culated and the hands continued to grab for more, one of the senior representatives approached me. 'Jonathan,' he said, 'I'll do whatever you need, I just want to help.' Amazing. We had hooked yet another one into our cause.

Jonathan's enthusiasm won over his school, student-by-student. Yet, until he made a personal appeal, the senior had been oblivious to the reasoning behind his posters and announcements. There was simply no substitute for a podium and close interaction.

Although some even robotically began Freedom's Answer as just another ordinary venture - by the end, it became blaringly real. Soham Dave, a Maryland student who spends his free time cruising in his 1991 Red Honda Civic, motored past indifference in one unique conversation. He offers details of the moment when he realized that our quest was larger than any scribbled name:

I saw him - at first, I barely noticed what color his jacket was, I barely noticed his worn face. But as I looked more deeply, and as he came closer, I noticed his jacket: green, torn with two patches. The first, a frayed and slightly faded profile of a bald eagle, majestically looked upwards with its wings outstretched. The other was new and alive, our Stars and Stripes. He finally reached our table and without saying a word, grabbed a pen. As he bent down to sign the pledge form, he raised his head, face bold with pride, eyes deep with feeling, and said, 'I came back in '72 after serving my country and hated everythin' about where this country was headin'. But you guys, there's somethin' in you - and for the first time in more than 30 years I'm gonna serve my country again.' He signed the pledge. It occurred to me as I stood there, how many millions of Americans had the tattered patch of patriotism close to their hearts and how many just needed one more stitch for that brand new patch. We are that stitch.

Each Freedom's Answer student had the ability to grasp, feel, and touch our creation, and together, in the final week, we heard the heartbeat. With every fresh idea, we added another level to that creation. And with every skeptic we proved wrong, we added emotion to it. We weren't sure of the possibilities, so we just did what we had always done. We kept on encouraging, assisting, and trying to outdo our friends.

The days came and went. It was now Sunday, a day of prayer and reflection for most of America. We reflected over the past months and prepared for the last two days ahead. Zach Clayton of North Carolina knew that his family and neighbors would be at church that Sunday and made one last stab at gaining other supporters.

My pastor had promised to talk about the importance of voting to our congregation on the Sunday before the election, so I decided to go down the street to another church and speak. It was Methodist; I was Presbyterian. It was black; I was white. Naturally, I felt hesitant, slightly uncomfortable as I approached the minister during 'pre-worship praise,' and asked him if I could speak to the congregation during the service. He glared at me, the outsider, denied me twice, then grudgingly relented when he realized I wouldn't give up.

'Make it quick,' he snapped before returning to prayer. Rarely nervous, I felt eyes peering into me as I took my seat on the bench by an elderly lady. Ten minutes into the service, I was introduced as a 'brother from White Memorial Church' and I stood up, swallowed, and spoke. 'Your children and

brothers are fighting for freedom, fighting for a
right - to vote - that some of us won't even use.
That's wrong,' I implored. Blunt, forward and fast I
continued with unremarkable words but remarkable
belief. Leaving the church afterwards, I was inun-
dated with responses, overwhelmed by people who
thanked me for the message. As I drove home, I
struggled to wipe the stupid grin off my face... all I
did was ask.

Sunday became Monday, a flurry of final neighborhood walks, reminder calls, posters, and newspaper articles. But before long, and after six long months of planning, we reached Election Day.

November 5, students served their country, not only by
delivering a record number of voters, but also by working
as poll workers. As one student poll worker from
Louisiana, Courtney, said, "I was actually part of the day,
not just a spectator. I saw it happen and noticed that people
cared." It wasn't like the mock election in debate class or
a vote in student council. This was something that we
could hold, touch, and feel. Trent Benishek, a poll worker
in Wisconsin, mentioned, "It's easy for a teacher to say that
people should vote on Election Day. But, actually seeing
Americans using that right was something that surpassed
any lesson in a classroom."

A sense of closure approached. We felt satisfied, but
were anxious to see promise in the results. Tyler White
reflected on Election Day:

Nervous anticipation twisted my stomach as I
watched CNN for initial voter turnout reports,
thinking to myself, 'Did we help accomplish the
impossible? Did I help spread democracy?' The television soon gave me a headache so I decided to

take a breather from politics and hit some golf balls at the driving range. I set up like usual, three balls on the right with the seven iron and driver ready. While I swung my seven iron, I noticed a kid who looked to be a freshman in high school eyeing the Freedom's Answer t-shirt I wore. He was more fixated on it than he was on the yellow golf ball lying on the ground in front of his feet. Finally, I asked him if we knew each other and he said, 'No, I don't believe we've met, but I am also a member of Freedom's Answer. I got my whole family to vote for the first time in their lives.' I stood there, nodded in time with the perfect breeze, and took a confident swing.

Throughout the pursuit, we had heard the cries from the sideline, cheering, inspiring, and motivating. They came from friends, family, colleagues, and those reaching for the same ribbon.

The Countdown

As we counted down to the day when we would watch election night news, we took heart in the inspiration that appeared in our email in-boxes from far-off allies. Dozens of final e-mails before Election Day reveal the story of the September 11 Generation's final sprint to the summit. Here are two:

Dane, Washington:

One week. Our time, effort and thought have all gone towards this next week. Will we make the goal? Will people respond? Was it all worth it? Although we will be asking ourselves these questions over the next few days, remember that it is more than that. It is showing our friends, our teachers, our communities, and our nation that we stand as a united group, committed to supporting democracy. It is realizing the true influence of youth in our society. Through our work, we have reminded people that their choice needs to be heard and as the student leaders of our country, we care that it is heard.

Josh, Maryland:

Six months ago, a few of us sat at the National Press Club and introduced the idea of Freedom's Answer to the world. What has occurred between now and then is nothing short of a phenomenon. In less than twelve hours all of your hard work, all of your hours spent on the phone and spent out in the cold getting pledges, will begin to pay off. It will be long remembered in history what a group of high school kids did to change the course of modern politics. And tomorrow, when all of this begins and ends, take a moment, take at least one moment, to reflect on the great masterpiece that all of us have created. Remember the way in which the students of America united, and remember how it all got started in the first place: A simple tribute to the victims of September 11.

Each voice was as an echo resounding through the canyons of our vast America. This voice, once unheard, was rising to a crescendo. But it wasn't always that way. Fourteen months earlier, we had paused in math class, blankly staring at live pictures from New York and Washington, not sure of what was coming next. In school, we are taught that we are the future. On 9-11, we weren't so sure that we wanted to be.

But we marched forward, planning blood drives and fundraisers, trying to do something, anything, significant. But nothing really sufficed. Scribbling letters to soldiers was fine and donating supplies was a valuable, but tentative, service. We searched for something that would bind together a wounded generation - and we found Freedom's Answer.

The day after the election, the experts were still crunching turnout numbers but there was already a sign in towns and cities across the country. Instead of dragging their heels as they got off the bus to watch MTV, kids in different states ripped through the newspaper, searching for voter results. We wanted to know. News anchors kept flipping through acceptance speeches, then finally, we got the message: we had done it. At first, the tallies were at "a little over 75 million." But in the end, close to 79 million votes were counted, crushing the national mid-term record and that of twenty-seven separate states.

We weren't oblivious. The population had grown, elections were close, and the political parties had done their automated phone calls and direct mail reminders. But those factors had always been there before. What hadn't? A million students on the street, reminding Americans that freedom isn't free.

Some jumped in exclamation, some wiped a tear, and some just smiled. The sacrifice paid off and oh, it felt good! For years, we had dreamt of a better system. That night, we had contributed to it.

We were all touched in a different way. Brad Moss, a computer junkie from Washington State who once was "apathetic, to say the least," had been drastically altered. That night, as he slouched under a hooded sweatshirt, lounging in his swivel chair, he reflected:

> Just a few short years ago, I dreamed of standing in
> front of the Presidential lectern and repeating the

famous phrase, 'My fellow Americans.' My mom even bought me a book entitled 'So you want to be the President.' I was a proud 'die-hard' political junkie with 'Republican' tendencies. But all that died. I became cynical and doubtful of democracy, of America, and of her dreams. In fact, I crawled into my digital hole and forgot all about my love for politics, the American dream and our principles - even those of just basic freedom. I became, simply put, indifferent.

But I am back. While I am still hopelessly stuck in my digital hole, my love of America and democracy has been refreshed, my hope renewed. I first started helping with Freedoms Answer because a friend asked me for help. I was swept up in the passion that was exhibited and perpetuated by this dynamic group. In short, I came in cynical and I left amazed, encouraged, and with a sense of hope for the future. I don't want to be the President anymore, nor do I have any party affiliation, but more importantly, I believe in America now.

We made history. This was our project, our legacy, and our call to arms. We couldn't fight overseas, but we could attack apathy at home. A record broken by over 3.5 million votes was a monument to freedom. America's youngest generation, the September 11 Generation, had begun to prove to ourselves that we would carry America through whatever she may face.

Zach Clayton concluded in a final email to the group he had helped form:

> Roughly four months ago we joined together, hoping to change America. Most of us still aren't old enough to vote, still aren't sure where we'll go to college, but already we have proved the pundits, pollsters, and pessimists wrong. We've broken the

voting record for a non-presidential election year!!

It began as a dream, and you've turned Freedom's Answer into reality. Never before have any of our organizations worked together, and the cooperation that has emerged from this endeavor speaks volumes about the strength of the idea, about the strength of your beliefs.

In our hearts we believed in something larger than any one of us, greater than any party or person - we believed in America as it can be, as it should be. For too long our generation has lacked real vision, has missed true leadership, has been blind to the possibility that our power can make a difference.

What have we learned? 2500 high schools and a million and more students want to believe that the America we will inherit can be stronger. We've taken ownership of a process and a project that has impacted millions and we have found that when we unite behind a common vision no obstacle can surmount the altruism and willingness to act that we've displayed.

The September 11 Generation might be the new kid on the block but we have just discovered that our voice certainly can be heard. My hope: it just keeps getting louder.

Throughout the course of history, when people believe deeply in an idea larger than themselves, they sacrifice anything to accomplish it. Secret Service agents take bullets, soldiers give their lives, the least we could do was make a stand. H.G. Wells once said, "The greatest task of democracy, its ritual and feast - is choice." We had stared the consequences of inaction in the eyes and chosen to fight back.

We are still new to the process; most of us weren't even 18 on Election Day. But we are ready to promise the nation that democracy will not die on our watch. Let the word go forth from here, the torch is now carried by a new generation. We will not stumble.

Freedom's Future

Chapter 7

In 2002 we wanted to make our own mark on the course of human events. We wanted to challenge America to hold onto that second moment of 9-11. We didn't end up rocking the country from top to bottom, but we did receive the attention of the national press, found a home in thousands of schools, and most importantly discovered that our generation is hungry. We learned how to lead and we shouldn't be shy about attempting to do more.

Helping to set a voter turnout record shows just how much power we have to shape our country's future to our dreams. That is the country's history, you know. From the first, it was the dreamers who shaped America, the dreamers who kept it alive, the dreamers who gave us that rebirth of freedom whenever the times demanded it.

America was once just such a dream. The British called it "dead-on-arrival," European monarchs scoffed at the notion of "rule by the people," and many of our own Americans denounced liberty as a pipe dream. A country anchored to the doctrines of an *idea!* The world had never seen anything like it before.

Then

Our forefathers refused to give up. They were relentless. Liberty wasn't about personal glory; it was about challenging a society to reinvent itself. There was something so seductive about pushing limits and watching them shatter, about opening the doors to the impossible.

Our founders, like many of us today, were disappointed with a system that ignored their voice. They fought furiously to change it, charging across uncharted territory, breaking past self-imposed boundaries to grasp their ideal: freedom. Others - scared to lose their power, position, and status, scared of change - condemned them, impeded them, even massacred them. The Patriots just fought harder. Virginia's Patrick Henry urged a resolution in Richmond supporting revolution after an excruciating back-and-forth debate:

> Mr. President...If we wish to be free, if we mean not to basely abandon the noble struggle in which we have been so long engaged... we must fight! I repeat it, sir, we must fight!
>
> They tell us, sir that we are weak - unable to cope with so formidable an adversary. But when shall we be stronger? Will it be the next week or the next year? Shall we gather strength by irresolution and inaction? Sir, we are not weak. Three millions of people, armed in the cause of liberty, and in such a country as that which we possess, are invincible by any force... Our brethren are already in the field! Why stand we here idle?

These young heroes of 1776, like 21 year-old Alexander Hamilton, were hardly older than us. Yet, they sacrificed their lives, they pledged their fortunes, they risked their honor to arouse a nation, to infect their fellow countrymen with a longing for equality. They recruited militias at nineteen, commanded armies at twenty-one, and were far "too naïve" to know that such a "young country could never possibly defeat a global power like Britain."

The general public wasn't asked to complain: they were asked to act! The common citizen was no longer a bystander in an aristocratic vie for power, because the power was already theirs. America took its first breath the moment it understood that a country is not made of its leaders - it's made of its people.

Ideals of freedom and democracy weren't new, but they were merely vague possibilities until the dreamers took up arms. Jefferson, Jay, Adams, Washington, and hundreds more, many times with their blood, drafted a frame to ensure that all Americans would enjoy the independence their fellow men had died for. But the greatest gift these giants bequeathed was flexibility. They looked to the future and didn't touch it. Thomas Jefferson:

> Each generation is as independent as the one preceding... It has then a right to choose for itself the form of government it believes most productive... to accommodate to the circumstances in which it finds itself... It is for the peace and good of mankind, that a solemn opportunity of doing this every 19 or 20 years, should be provided in the constitution, so that it may be handed on, with periodic repairs, from generation to generation, to the end of time.

The signers of the Constitution fashioned a creation larger than any man - even a king. Their fantastic "experiment in democracy" would respond to change, ensuring young dreamers could push us forward. They imagined that each new generation would redefine freedom in their own terms for their own times.

Now

Fast-forward 227 years. What happened? We're no longer standing atop fish barrels in the harbor, pleading with our fellow man like Thomas Paine. We're stuck inside watching a television set that tells us how to think. Our founders established government to, "provide for the common defense, promote the general welfare, and secure the blessings of liberty..." Until 1920, that meant relatively little help to or interference with American citizens. We spent about 3% of national income on government without entitlements, social welfare, or income re-distribution.

The times have drastically changed. Uncle Sam's functions have been greatly expanded to encompass massive programs like Social Security, Medicare, and Welfare in an effort to meet human needs on an individual level and solve umbrella-type social problems.

Democrats argue that our society has become more humane, Republicans complain that typical Americans pay more in taxes than they do on food, shelter and clothing combined. But the stark truth? Our generation stands to inherit massive problems from both parties - a colossal national debt, a struggling educational system, an ongoing war on terror, and more - crying out for Jefferson's refined definition of American freedom.

America's New Face

Older. People now live much, much longer than they used to. Long-term care is a real issue that every family and the society have to confront. Retirement keeps coming earlier and death later. Somebody has to be responsible for what happens in between. Easy question: How do we best use the time of able-bodied retirees who want to volunteer? Tough question: How do we meet a collective responsibility to provide life with dignity for those who are incapable of most things but still alive? It's a question that only a very rich society would ever worry about, but that is what we are.

Diverse. We call ourselves a melting pot. People are more multi-cultured and get along better here than anywhere else in the world. But are we one society? Lines drawn in the sand still separate us. Language is the most obvious. It once seemed the only practical requirement of becoming an American and pursuing your dream was to learn the language. But the most rapidly growing segment of the population doesn't speak the same language as the rest do. So do we adjust to a new reality or seek to hold on to the old? The other generations have ignored the changing sound of America. We can't.

Bigger. When the constitution was signed, our population was 3.8 million. Last year alone, our population grew 3.1 million. Representative democracy becomes more difficult when the political leadership is required to represent so many people. How are the precious concepts of individual freedom and opportunity best served when legislation and regulation lump more and more people into easy-to-manage pigeonholes? The larger the groups the less individual differences seem to matter - yet freedom above all means the right to be different.

Distant. Community in the time of the founding fathers meant who lived next door, who you went to school with, who you sold your farm produce to, and the friends you saw at church. You didn't chat online in a virtual community or schedule coffee fifteen minutes away at Starbucks; you walked across the street to your neighbor's parlor. Other states were weeks away and close relatives, who moved away, were no longer close. Today, we know more about the President than the guy who lives in the house on the corner. The world is at the doorstep every night, while the neighbor's kid sells Girl Scout cookies at your doorstep only once a year. Re-capturing for America that spirit of community - of love and compassion - that define the September 11 Generation is one of the most daunting tasks at hand. Why does it seem to take falling buildings and a war before we reach out to one another?

Faster. Televised communications are now worldwide in real color and real time. Forget "American Idol" and "Joe Millionaire." Television in high definition and real time is the real reality TV. Vietnam, while in color, was reported in packaged segments, taped first and then broadcast delayed. The Challenger exploded live, but the "close-ups" came well after the voice-over reports. Now the events, reporting, and "expert" judgments are all instantaneous. Leaders must react virtually in the open, with little time to think before they speak. "Let me think about that before I say anything," is considered an unacceptable answer.

This changing composition of our nation offers incredible possibilities. Unfortunately, it has also given rise to new problems. Like today's America, our new problems are bigger and faster and continue to grow.

America's New Problems

The Gap. Our poor are the most well off in the history of the world. In most other countries, they would be among the richest. But that doesn't mean that America's gap between rich and poor isn't growing every day, especially among our newest Hispanic immigrants. Will the gap foster unintended, but very real, racial tension?

Medical Discoveries. While modern medical science has given us increased longevity and victory over once fatal diseases, it brings other implications as well. Where do we draw the line between funding the young's education and funding the old's health care? Whether cloning *should* happen can yield a simple moral answer, but it *will* happen. What should be done about it? Will clones be free people?

Superpower Status. Since 9/11, we can't safely ignore anything that goes on in the world. And because no one rivals our economic wealth or military strength, do we have a responsibility to act if a danger is posed to us or anybody else? What are the lines we will cross? What are the lines we won't?

Security. And where do we draw the lines at home? Should the Department of Homeland Security, a likely target of terror itself, be headquartered in Washington? Does that invite catastrophe? And what rights should we willingly give up to achieve security through increased surveillance by the government?

National Debt. The generation that created a national debt of $7 trillion has zero plans to pay it. Those who vote most, seniors, won't be around long enough to worry about dealing with the burden. We will.

Status-quo Education. Despite increased spending, many of our teachers gripe more and teach less, while many of our peers still board the bus to inner-city hellholes. The Internet has forced the business world to live on speed. But elements of society, like government, that aren't based on the profit motive - that don't have to respond to reality or die - have not kept pace. Public education, by and large, while changing, is still falling farther behind the curve every year. And it feeds that gap between rich and poor even further. But can we afford to spend still more and build the debt still larger? Can we afford not to?

Social Security. What started as a supplement to seniors' income now is a "right" all seniors feel they have earned. And as more Boomers retire, the cost of funding their "golden years" will increase dramatically. Need that be at the expense of education or the young?

Not one of these questions is easy. None will answer themselves. But they are the issues left on our plate. We didn't create them; we inherited them.

The Greatest Problem

New frightening challenges will continue to land on our doorstep, but the most scary reality is that politics today - the system through which we deal with our gravest national questions - reflects a sad evolution of a once brave dream. How can we debate real solutions in sixty-second "news updates?" How can TV shouting matches substitute for serious discourse? How will we recapture the broad and sweeping dialogue that once helped craft vision?

Politics is seldom seen as an honor anymore. In the nation's eyes, D.C. seems an incurable center of self-interest - a disconnected, distant inheritance of the selfless public service about which our nation's founders dreamed. Once upon a time, the honor of public service was what we bestowed upon the greatest leaders of the day. America's best scientists, farmers, inventors, and businessmen occupied our marble halls, and openly debated the country's pressing problems.

Now, we're barraged with jokes and late night monologues about our elected officials. We watch a self-righteous press provide instant replays of our leaders' every misstep and we wonder why the quality of public service has declined. As one former state legislator told us, "The best and brightest are no longer easily or automatically drawn to public service or politics. Optimistic can-do people just don't want to subject themselves to grueling campaigns and negative attacks, while simultaneously begging their friends and colleagues for money to fill people's mailboxes." Politics subjects those who pursue it, and their families, to a life of invasion and negative attacks that turn most good people away.

Some idealistic hometown heroes run campaigns with a deep-rooted belief that, "Washington is a perplexing place, but I can change it. I can make it work." Once elected, they depart for Congress, aspiring to transform government. But more often than not, before the end of their third term D.C. captures them. They come to Washington eager to represent Pocatello, but now when they're back in Idaho, they represent Washington to Pocatello instead.

Our founders never planned for Congress or the State House to be full-time jobs. Not too long ago, politicians were citizen-legislators who farmed during the summer and came to Washington or the state capitols for a few months during the winter to pass legislation and go home. Certainly our society has become more complex and difficult, requiring longer and perhaps continuous legislative sessions. But how can career politicians, living full-time in Washington, hope to represent people who live full-time back home?

Here We Go.

The nation is looking for answers - the nation is looking for the next great leaders to rise and speak. It is a chance for us to demand change, an obligation to come of age. We can ignore pressing national issues and pretend our political frustrations will pass or we can stand resolute. Don't be intimidated. Just think of this as another frontier to conquer, another impossibility that we can make possible, a series of extraordinary opportunities.

Young people are no less capable of genius, invention and leadership now than ever before. Alexander the Great conquered the known world before 29; the average age at the Constitutional Convention was 36; Emerson graduated from Harvard at 14. As tough as the problems we face may be, we must address them, and in doing so the September 11 Generation can help invigorate a worn-out system. The course of our nation and our future is largely dependent on the choice we make, the choice before you on this very page. Will you join us?

Looking through that lens of the second moment of 9/11, we witnessed the potential of what our country could be. We saw men and women and children care about each other's future, we saw an outpouring of humanity, and an honest interest in how to move forward as one nation. We want that back. We want to re-capture that moment and make it permanent.

The headquarters of the effort will be a new home-page for our generation: **www.september11genera-tion.org.** It was made for you. All that we ask is that you come and you make it yours. We'll have weekly "fire-site" chats, where you'll hear from our generation's leaders. We'll talk about issues that Washington won't touch and ideas it doesn't debate. The decisions

Washington makes or ducks today will impact us years after its politicians are no longer with us. We need to be heard on anything that will affect our lives.

When our older brothers and sisters chose to walk away from a political system that they did not like or trust, they gave up the chance for their views to be heard. Those who are part of the political system - those who produce votes, as we just did - those are the players at the table. We have earned the right; we have the political influence to be heard. We have the power to change what we don't like.

www.september11generation.org is our chance to be at the table when history is written; it's a national campfire for the nation's youngest leaders. It can be our forum, our debating hall, our megaphone. Generational news, heroes of the week, message boards, weekly columns and stories, and hot topics will all be featured. Join us for live chats and Q & As, post your ideas and success stories, and get help when you are frustrated. A library of tools, like sample press releases, action steps, and speeches, will be supplemented by "e-tutors" who will advise you if you run into trouble. We'll decipher political issues with straightforward pros and cons and provide you access to politicians in Washington so your voice can be heard.

In 2002 with Freedom's Answer, we involved just a fraction of America's high schools and students. There are more than 15 million high school students in America. Imagine what can happen in 2004. Imagine what can happen in a year! The next time America goes to the polls, the next time America elects its

President, is the next time we have the chance to prove that we're serious. We're not going away.

We want to register every new voter we can locate and turn out every vote we find. You'll recognize some familiar political faces and some celebrities too. While on the ground we ask for pledges, register voters, plan rallies, and startle politicians with our presence; air cover will include broad media exposure through the key fall months before November.

We will be all over this election. Freedom's Answer will be on your radio, in your newspaper, and plastered on your TV. We will recruit national marketing sponsors who will infiltrate every aspect of American culture, whether you're sitting on your couch watching ridiculous campaign commercials or walking through Times Square. We'll also expand web coverage, celebrity endorsements, and sitcom script mentions. You will even find us at the polls on Election Day, inside as poll workers and outside as greeters. We will be inescapable. It will be symbolic of the revolution the September 11 Generation will lead. Words like "democracy" and "liberty" will breathe new life. We have an unparalleled opportunity to rewrite the meaning of freedom on the hearts of our generation. We have a chance to make America stand taller.

We're tired of being cynical. We're sick of being ignored. We're scared at what will happen if we don't speak up. So what we're attempting to do is nothing short of incredible. You ready? The countdown has already started; the eyes are already on us. People are staring at America's students in disbelief, and it's time for us to astonish them. We're asking you to get up, we're asking you to stand with us, we're asking you to dream. We are asking. Will you answer?

Acknowledgements

We are indebted to all the students of Freedom's Answer who gave voice to our generation through their stories (included in this text and not), their insights, their advice, and most importantly, their leadership.

We are grateful for two cheerful and capable friends, Pat Miller and Liz Mclean, who supplied extraordinary logistical assistance. Their constant willingness to lend a hand helped us meet impossible deadlines. We were fortunate to have the sound advice of the organization's professional staff of Jim Jonas, Ted McConnell, Jenna Hamrick-Young, and Karla Johnson-Grimes. We also appreciate the advice, recollections, and editorial comments of Betsy White, Communications Director of Freedom's Answer. *Peak Creative Services,* a skilled and generous Denver firm who managed the Freedom's Answer website and constructed **www.september11generation.org,** designed the book cover.

A.P. Carlton Jr., President of the American Bar Association, Rocco Marano of The National Association of Secondary School Principals, and Kris Minor of America's Promise, provided remarkable support for Freedom's Answer through their respective organizations. No three adults were more essential to our success in 2002. We also thank Alan Head and the North Carolina Bar Association for donating exceptional facilities for our revision sessions.

The editorial suggestions of Phil Longman, Neil Howe, and Chris Arterton were invaluable at the eleventh hour. We also thank Senator and Mrs. Richard Stevens for their keen eyes. Harriett Hill provided perceptive advice and a methodical review of the drafts. And we are additionally grateful to our informal focus group of student readers who reviewed the text and offered criticism.

The timely advance printing of this book would not have been possible without the expertise, common sense, efficiency, and good humor of the late Todd Miller who represented Production Solutions Inc.

Ellen Reid, a skilled and experienced publisher, shepherded this edition to a quick publication. We all appreciate her time, dedication, and incredible energy. Her team included Laren Bright, an Emmy-nominated writer, who brilliantly suggested our subtitle, "When the Twin Towers fell, the next generation rose!" The phrase was a powerful way to convey the hope we have in our future, the idealism we witnessed during the Second Moment of 9-11, and the promise of the September 11 Generation.

This book and the accomplishments it highlights would have not been possible without two unparalleled advisors, Mike McCurry and Doug Bailey, honorary members of the September 11 Generation. Thank you for your wise counsel, open-minds, and giving hearts.

Finally, we extend our deep appreciation to teachers, family, and friends who have so strongly supported our efforts throughout the past eight months. You is off the heezy fo sheezy.

What's Next?

If you think that this book should be the first chapter in the future of our country, join us.

Visit our websites at:

www.September11Generation.org and
www.FreedomsAnswer.org

Email us at info@freedomsanswer.org

Write us at Freedom's Answer, 1233 20th Street, NW, #206, Washington, DC, 20036

Even call us at 202/785-5920

We'd love to have your hands and heart involved with our work and we also welcome your tax-deductible donations to the "Freedom's Answer Foundation." Funds support the distribution of this book to American high school students, maintenance of our websites, and the continuation of the Freedom's Answer program.

We hope to hear from *you*.